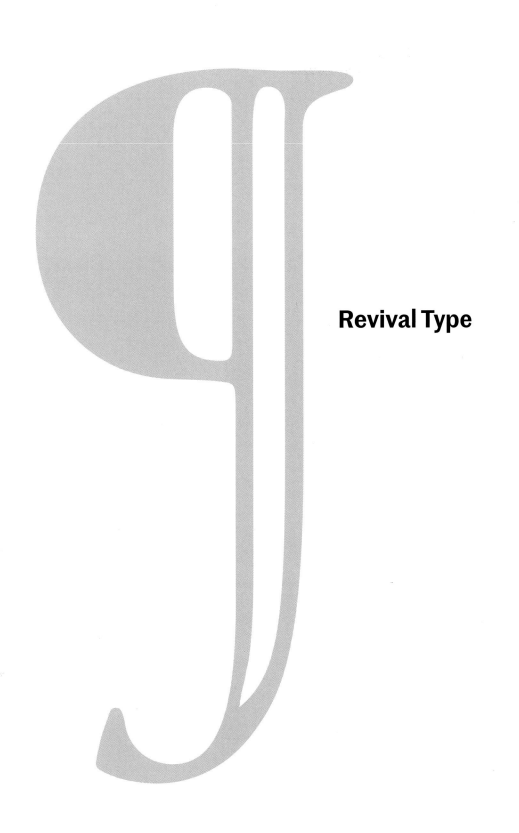

Revival Type

REVIVAL TYPE

Digital typefaces inspired by the past

Paul Shaw

Foreword by Jonathan Hoefler

Yale University Press

PILCROWS

half title | LTC Goudy Oldstyle Pro
title | Marr Sans
Contents | Brunel Deck
Foreword | Quarto
Introduction | Big Caslon
Inscriptional Letters | Capitolium
Blackletter | Flamande
Venetian Oldstyle & Aldine Types | Abrams Venetian
French Oldstyle Types | Garamond Premier Pro
Dutch Oldstyle Types | Renard No. 1
Transitional Types | PS Fournier Pro Grand
Neoclassical Types | Linotype Didot
Fat Faces | Big Figgins
Slab Serifs | OL Egiziano Classic
Wood Type | HWT Tuscan Extended
Late Victorian Types | Kolo OT
20th Century Seriffed Types | Palatino Nova
Grotesques & Gothics | Marr Sans
Geometric Sans Serifs | DTL Nobel
Humanist Sans Serifs | Optima Nova
Scripts | ITC Mistral Light

Published in North America in 2017 by
Yale University Press
302 Temple Street
P.O. Box 209040
New Haven, CT 06520-9040
yalebooks.com/art

Conceived, designed, and produced by
Quid Publishing, Part of the Quarto Group
Ovest House, 58 West Street
Brighton BN1 2RA
United Kingdom

Book design by Abby Goldstein and Paul Shaw

Printed in China
ISBN 978-0-300-21929-6

Library of Congress Control Number: 2016955720

A catalogue record for this book is available from the British Library.

The paper in this book meets the requirements of ANSI/NISO Z39.48-1992 (Permanence of Paper).

10 9 8 7 6 5 4 3 2 1

FRONTISPIECE: Detail of Caslon English Italian punches. Photograph by John Bodkin.

LEFT: Detail of proof of Monotype Centaur (9 November 1928) with annotations by Bruce Rogers.

Contents

~: Ludouicus Vicentin. ſcribebat :~

+ Rome anno domini +

• MDXXII •

Foreword

¶ Is any typeface a revival? Isn't every typeface a revival?

To a typeface designer, the gravitational pull of history is inescapable. Even the creator of a progressive, original font has to contend with readers' interpretations of what letterforms are supposed to mean, expectations that are shaped by centuries of communication through type. Typefaces signal whether a movie is a romantic comedy or a horror flick; whether its heroes will be kids, soldiers, models, athletes, robots, or knights. In many ways, every typeface must be historical. The "historical revival" is typography's most explicit way of working with traditional forms. In a revival, a designer takes on specific historical artifacts, and attempts to capture their essence in a functional font. Revivals can be strict recreations, oblique interpretations, or even works of satire. Yet compared with other arts, typeface design has a frustrating paucity of language to describe these differences. A portrayal of *Hamlet* is understood to be a performance, not an imitation, and to recast the story in an unusual setting is recognized as an original act that adds to the text, rather than diminishing it. Architects distinguish between renovation and conservation projects; musicians have "based on a theme by," as well as remixes, samples, and mashups. Typographic revivals can take many paths, none of them well marked, but all of them sharing the goal of adding something new and unique to the corpus.

In this book, Paul Shaw presents a collection of such projects that exhibit a wide range of different approaches. He introduces useful definitions that are inclusive, not doctrinaire, and designed to reveal the process by which these faces came to be. This is a typographic tour told through astute profiles that highlight the distinctions and merits of different designs, and together illuminate one of typography's most cherished treasures, its living history.

JONATHAN HOEFLER
Founder, H&Co
October 2016

OPPOSITE: Detail of f.11v from *La Operina di Ludovico Vicentino, da imparare di scriuere littera cancellarescha* by Ludovico Vicentino degli Arrighi (Rome: 1522 [1524]).

S. Sebastiano

Introduction

TYPE REVIVALS: COPIES, MODELS AND MUSES

Revival Type: Digital Typefaces Inspired by the Past is an overview of the various ways in which lettering and typefaces from the past have provided inspiration for contemporary type designers.

The idea of reviving a typeface from the past has been a contentious one. Modernists have argued that designers should use the typefaces of their own time. Reviving older typefaces is viewed as an exercise in nostalgia. But if we embrace the modernist argument we would be continually having to make new typefaces. How do we define "our time"? Is it a year, a decade, a generation? Typefaces (and letters in general) are an essential element of our culture manifested in documents, books, and ephemera. They are part of a historical continuum that remains the same even as it constantly changes. The best typefaces are as much a part of the 21st century as of the age when they were created. They transcend time and place.

WHAT IS A REVIVAL?

The notion of a type revival is more complex than it seems at first glance. The digital type "revivals" that exist today go beyond the straightforward idea of taking a typeface from the pre-digital past and converting it into pixels for use on computers and mobile devices. Some designs are not revivals of typefaces *per se* but of letterforms, from inscriptions to calligraphic manuals to lettering in posters, bookjackets and other ephemera. Some revivals are aesthetic extensions or reimaginings of 20th-century typefaces occasioned by the need to update them technically. And others are actually reinterpretations or variations of typefaces from the past necessitated by having to make types that function in the 21st century and not in the distant past.

In this book, a type revival is broadly defined as a typeface whose characters are derived from a previous typeface or example of lettering. The many kinds of type revivals can be plotted along a spectrum from facsimiles to experimental designs.

OPPOSITE: Detail of rubbing by Paul Shaw (2013) of Damasian capitals from inscription (366–384 AD) in San Sebastiano fuori le Mura in Rome. These letters were the inspiration for Philocalus by Garrett Boge (LetterPerfect, 1997).

TYPES OF TYPE REVIVALS

The simplest and purest kind of type revival is a facsimile. A facsimile aims to reproduce as exactly as possible, without any alteration or improvement, the appearance of a typeface or set of letters from the past in a contemporary technological format. Frequently, it includes archaic letterforms and other characters while lacking some of those (e.g., currency symbols) that are essential for communication today. There are no pure facsimiles in this book. Both Architype Bayer (p. 213) and Architype Renner (p. 215), with their limited character sets, come close. But the letters that both are based on have been carefully massaged to convert them into visually cohesive and consistent typefaces. At first glance, several of the wood types (e.g., Cottonwood p. 147) as well as the blackletter designs Alter Littera Gutenberg B by José Alberto Mauricio (b. 1965) (p. 35) and Flamande by Matthew Carter (b. 1937) (p. 37) appear to be facsimiles, but their character sets contain several altered letters as well as additional ones not present in their models. True facsimiles are only of use to antiquarians and academic specialists.

Many type revivals aim to be historically authentic while being technologically up-to-date. They walk a tightrope between these two competing ideals.

A box of punches cut by Giambattista Bodoni. Photograph by Paul Shaw, 2008.

The impetus for such designs is a desire to resuscitate a typeface or letterform that is aesthetically appealing but technically unavailable, to make it a part of the present as well as of the past by giving it digital form. Some revivals in this mode include archaic characters (e.g., long **s**) while others jettison them. But all have augmented character sets required for contemporary functionality. Examples of this category are Donatello (p. 29) and Adobe Jenson Pro (p. 43). Some type revivals are concerned with matching their models as closely as possible while adapting them to current technology. Others are more interested in simply capturing the spirit of their models and reinventing them for new uses and situations. Adobe Garamond Premier Pro (pp. 53, 55 and 57) is an example of the first approach while Quarto (p. 77) represents the second view.

Type revivals are not always a one-to-one proposition in which a typeface or alphabet from the past is translated letter by letter, character by character to a digital format. Instead, some are synthesized from several models that have the desired spirit but each of which, for various reasons, is insufficient or imperfect. For instance, HTF Didot (p. 111) is not based on a single typeface but on a group of them that share the "Didot" sensibility, including some cut by punchcutters other than Firmin Didot. Similarly, Adobe Caslon (p. 83) is an interpretation of Caslon-ness derived from six text sizes of Caslon types.

Toward the other end of the spectrum from the facsimiles and historically authentic type revivals are type designs that simply use the types of the past as an inspiration for a variant design or a jumping off point for a new design. For instance, Mrs. Eaves (p. 97) and Filosofia (p. 107) are both deliberate attempts to make new typefaces that contain some of the DNA of historical types—in this case, those of Baskerville and Bodoni respectively—without being clones. Even further away from its source is Arbor (p. 125), which has used the bizarre Caslon Italian typeface as the springboard for an entirely new design that manages to be harmonious and legible by ignoring those aspects of the older design that are impractical

TOP: A punch and a matrix for capital **R** from the box of punches on the opposite page. Photographs by Paul Shaw, 2008.
ABOVE: Doves Press roman type recovered from the Thames River in 2014 by Robert Green. Photograph by Robert Green, 2014.

or just plain weird. The Marian family of typefaces, of which only Marian 1554 Italic (p. 59) is included here, is a revival of another kind: an experimental dissection of several types of the past as a form of structural analysis. It can be best described as a revival of the "bones" of typefaces rather than of their spirit.

Many typefaces of the 20th century (e.g., Times Roman) have continually been adapted to new type formats as technology has changed from foundry to machine composition to film composition to digital. Those that have been updated technologically but not aesthetically have been excluded from this book. However, the handful that have been reassessed, redesigned and extended as part of an upgrade to the latest digital format *are* of interest. Some, such as Palatino Nova (pp. 171 and 173) and Frutiger Serif (p. 187), have involved their original designers. But others have invited criticism as contemporary designers try to "improve" a typeface from the recent past while staying true to the aesthetic of the original designer. This is the case with Cartier (p. 175) and Sabon Next (p. 61).

THE CHALLENGES OF MAKING TYPE REVIVALS

The diverse range of type revivals is a reflection of differing views about what constitutes a type revival and how it should be done, as well as the nature of the

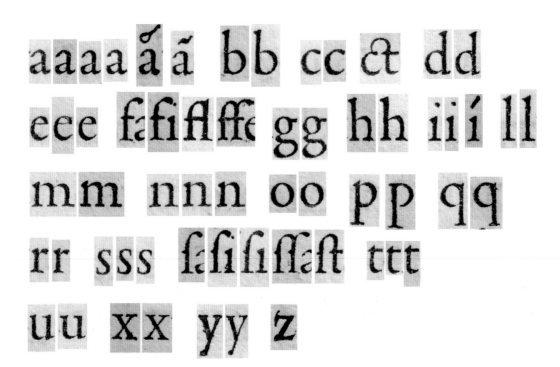

Inventory of letters from R9 type by Francesco Griffo compiled by Riccardo Olocco, *De Aetna* (1495).

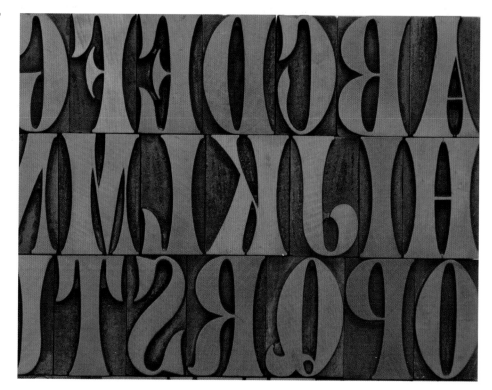

source material. Among the items used by contemporary designers as resources and inspiration are inscriptions, manuscripts, punches and matrices, metal or wood type, drawings, and printed items (books, type specimens, proofs, and ephemera). All of these sources are represented by the typefaces in this book.

Each of these sources has its advantages and drawbacks. The revival of a metal typeface created before the 1880s is dependent on punches, matrices, types or printed exemplars (either in books or type specimens). Types from long ago have rarely survived, but some punches and matrices have. These can provide precise models. The principle drawback is that many of the characters needed for a modern fount of type are lacking and have to be invented. Renard (p. 75) by Fred Smeijers (b. 1961) is a typeface whose design is based on surviving punches and matrices in the Plantin-Moretus Museum in Antwerp, proofs made from castings of the matrices, along with Smeijers' own attempts to learn the art of punchcutting.

When punches and matrices are non-existent, designers have to rely on printed specimens of types for their models. These require more interpretation as the impression of the type can vary greatly within a page depending on the skill of the printer. Ink squash needs to be taken into account in trying to discern the true

ABOVE: Painter's Roman (1870s) wood type. This cut matches Seven Line No. 110 in *Specimens of Machine Cut Wood Type! Manufactured by The Wm. H. Page Wood Type Co.* (Norwich, Connecticut, 1888).
COMPARISON (ABOVE LEFT): AI Wood Painter by Peter Fraterdeus (Alphabets, Inc., 1992) vs. Juniper by Joy Redick (Adobe, 1989).

form of the typeface. Whether the punchcutter anticipated ink squash is a matter of debate. This was the problem Mark van Bronkhorst (b. 1965) faced in designing MvB Verdigris Italic (p. 63) solely from a typeface in a printed book.

Along with ink squash, designers trying to revive metal typefaces are also confronted with the problem of size. Before the invention of the Benton punch-cutting machine in the early 1880s, all metal types varied in design from size to size. Choosing the right point size as a model is often crucial. In the work of most punchcutters the variations are slight, but important. These variations include optical adjustments such as changes in the x-height and width of letters, the thickness of thin strokes, the size of counters, and the deletion of decorative details necessary to make typefaces legible at small sizes. Subtleties such as these are behind the design of Adobe Garamond Premier Pro (pp. 53, 55 and 57). Sometimes the differences among sizes are more structural. This is especially true of the Caslon types and explains why there are several competing approaches to making a modern Caslon type. See ITC Founder's Caslon (pp. 81 and 82), Big Caslon (pp. 82 and 83) and Adobe Caslon (p. 83).

Surviving wood type is often warped, cracked or nicked. For graphic designers this is its charm, but for type designers bent on making a digital revival these are all obstacles—unless the goal is a distressed typeface. Wood type presents other problems since it was intended primarily for broadsides. Character sets are

American Type Founders pantographic pattern plate for 24 pt. Caslon 540 Italic.

severely limited with only a few having lowercase letters; and letters tend to be very large. Reviving wood type involves adjusting serifs, crotches, junctures, counters, and decorative elements so that letters can function adequately at the smaller sizes required for most designs. For examples of such adjustments, see Poplar (p. 155) and Pepperwood (p. 151).

Although most wood type revivals rely on the pioneering work of Rob Roy Kelly, author of *American Wood Type, 1828–1900* (1969), others increasingly look to the wood itself. Like foundry type, wood type was commonly pirated and identifying the originator of a particular design is difficult. Designs that superficially seem the same often have a few characters that differ. This explains why competing digital revivals of wood type are not identical (e.g., HWT Roman Extended Fatface and Madrone, p. 137).

Not all type revivals derive from type, whether metal or wood. Instead many are increasingly inspired by letterforms that have never existed as type: inscriptions, calligraphy, drawn lettering, handwriting, graffiti, and so on. In these manual sources there is far more variation in form than is found in early typefaces, making the task of selecting the right instances more daunting—even with the OpenType option of creating contextual alternates. P22 Operina (p. 237), Bickham Script (p. 239) and Burgues Script (p. 241) all show how open-ended and complex types based on calligraphic models can be.

As with wood type, designers seeking to revive inscriptional letters need to take into account the immense change in scale. But they also need to account for the difference between letters having dimensionality based on light, shadow and depth, and type that is black and white. Furthermore, photographs of inscriptions are weak as source material because letters are often distorted due to parallax. Rubbings are free from such problems, but they are frequently difficult to make since inscriptions (with the notable exception of gravestones and tombs) tend to be positioned high above the ground. Both Adobe Trajan (p. 21) and Donatello (p. 29) relied on rubbings as source material. Finally, inscriptions are almost always composed in capitals, requiring many characters to be invented wholesale if a fully functional typeface is the goal. This can be a formidable task, though not impossible as evidenced by HTF Requiem (p. 27).

Converting lettering into a typeface is often more difficult even than reviving a calligraphic hand, since individual letters are usually designed to fit a specific layout. They are joined in ligatures, reduced in size to nest within letters, distorted to fit the space available between adjacent letters, and elongated to fill out lines or the space between lines. All of this is the opposite of the goal in type design where each letter is designed to fit comfortably between every possible permutation of two letters. In such a situation extracting individual letters from their original context and altering them so that they can function in multiple situations without a significant loss of character is a challenge. Examples of typefaces that have successfully managed to do this include Kolo (p. 161), ITC Rennie Mackintosh (p. 163), and Mostra Nuova (p. 225).

SOME NOTES ON THIS BOOK

Revival Type is organized chronologically but it is not a history of type. For the most part, typefaces have been grouped using venerable classification categories that are easily understandable, even if they may dismay those who desire precision and consistency. A few categories (e.g., Late Victorian Types) have been invented to group disparate typefaces that would otherwise have been stranded on their own. These categories provide the organizational structure for *Revival Type*, with each chapter containing typefaces within that style. The chapters open with an introductory text summarizing the history of that particular category—emphasizing calligraphers, punchcutters, printers, publishers, and other significant individuals—as a background to the profiles of typeface revivals that follow. Shorter texts for each typeface then describe the lettering or historic typeface it is modeled on, summarize how it came into being, and present some of the problems involved in making it. Key characters are highlighted, and an overall assessment is provided.

The structure of *Revival Type* is simple. For each typeface highlighted in the book there is a sample of the lettering or historic typeface behind it, a showing of its basic character set (at 27 pt except for several wood types that are at 54 pt), and a comparison between the typeface (indicated in vermilion) and the model using enlarged letters from the latter. Sometimes, distinctive letters from the revived typeface (indicated in gray) have also been enlarged for closer examination. Several punchcutters from the past (e.g., Garamont, Caslon and Didot) have inspired multiple revivals. In those instances, cross-comparisons among competing revivals (e.g., Linotype Didot, HTF Didot, and LP Didot) and the original design have also been made.

The basic character sets for each typeface include capitals, small capitals, lowercase, oldstyle, and lining figures, basic punctuation, swash letters, alternates, ligatures (except dipthongs and eszett), and, in some instances, ornaments. The only typefaces that are not complete in this manner are Bickham Script and

Burgues Script, which have enormous glyph sets that could not be fitted into the layout of *Revival Type*. Accented characters and Greek and Cyrillic extensions have been excluded.

The number of type revivals has been growing exponentially over the past quarter century—with new releases continually begging to be added to *Revival Type* even as the book was in progress—making the selection process extremely difficult. The typefaces that made the cut were chosen because they represent a wide range of typographic history, exemplify many of the obstacles involved in creating a revival, were based on unusual source material (e.g., a Renaissance engraving, 19th- century stencil punches, and highway signage), and display a variety of

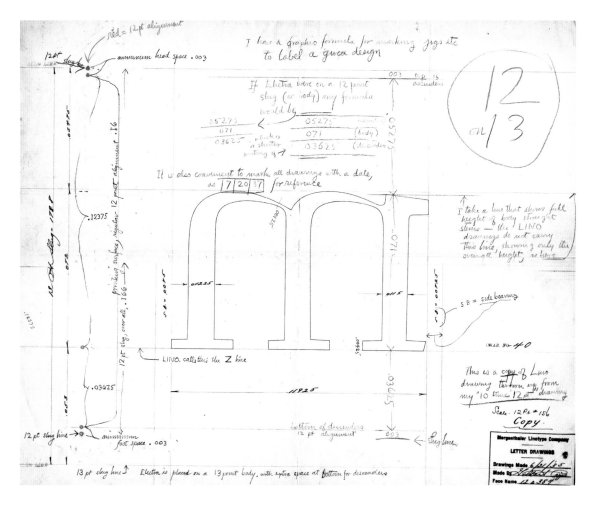

Mergenthaler Linotype drawing of Electra **m** (1935) with annotations by W.A. Dwiggins (1937) intended for Rudolph Ruzicka.

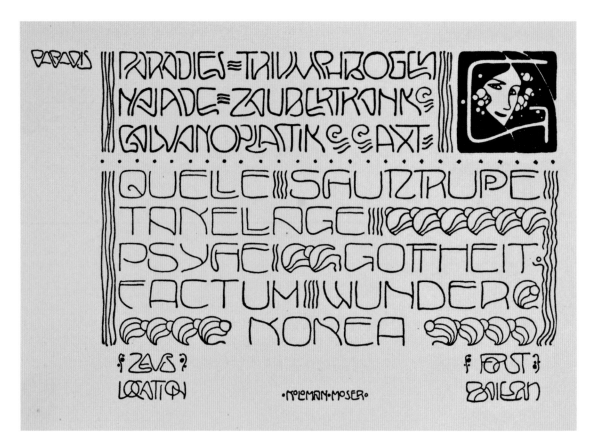

philosophical approaches to the concept of a type revival. All of them are digital originals rather than mere technological updates of revivals originally made in the metal or phototype eras. (Thus, there is no Bembo, Janson Text, or ITC Cheltenham). And all of the typefaces are commercially available. Fascinating revivals created as custom fonts (e.g., Empire State Building [2007] by Christian Schwartz and Paul Barnes, St. Bart's [2011] by Jesse Ragan, or Grolier [2015] by Jerry Kelly) have been excluded. The final list of typefaces in *Revival Type* encompasses modern classics (e.g., Adobe Trajan, p. 21, Mrs. Eaves, p. 96, and Miller, p. 119), cult favorites (e.g., Renard, p. 75 and MvB Verdigris, p. 63), overlooked gems (e.g., Brunel, p. 119), innovative interpretations (e.g., Arbor, p. 125) and experimental designs (e.g., Marian, p. 59). The selection ranges from the wonderful to the weird.

This introduction is followed by a section on typeface terminology. It is broader than most in order to provide a basis for understanding the wide range of type-faces covered in *Revival Type*. The numerous terms are illustrated exclusively with typefaces profiled in the book.

Lettering by Koloman Moser from *Beispiele Künstlerische Schrift* vol. 1 by Rudolf von Larisch (Vienna: Verlag Anton Schroll & Co., 1900).

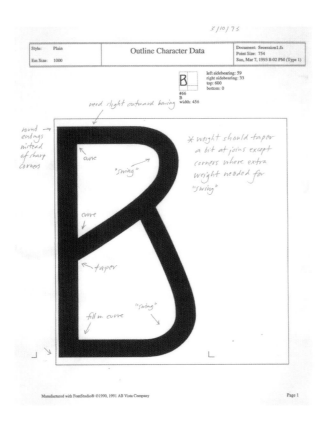

A FINAL NOTE ON TYPE REVIVALS

Revival Type has stretched the notion of what a revival is with its inclusion of loose reinterpretations such as Arbor and historical riffs like Marian alongside the expected types based on Jenson, Garamont, Caslon, Baskerville, Bodoni, and Didot. The intent has been to encourage graphic designers to think both more broadly and more deeply about revivals; to go beyond an assessment of them based solely on their historic authenticity or fidelity and to consider the intentions behind the typeface as well as its expected function. By including multiple typefaces derived from the same source or similar sources, *Revival Type* also hopes to spur graphic designers to discover alternatives to the classic or popular typefaces that so often become default choices. Instead of Baskerville, try Austin; or substitute DTL Nobel for Futura. Experiment and explore.

The typefaces in *Revival Type* are a reminder that the past is always present. Embrace it.

A Font Studio laser print, with annotations by Paul Shaw (1993), showing Outline Character Data for Kolo **B**. Digitization by Garrett Boge.

PLAN OF CASES,

ADAPTED TO

EDMUND FRY AND SON'S

Great Primer Script.

Type Street, 1821.

Terminology

SERIF   SANS SERIF   BLACKLETTER

ROMAN   ITALIC

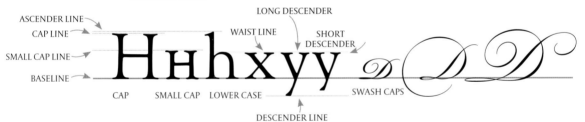

POINTED PEN SCRIPT   HANDWRITING

CHANCERY ITALIC

ASCENDER LINE
CAP LINE
SMALL CAP LINE
BASELINE

LONG DESCENDER
WAIST LINE
SHORT DESCENDER

CAP   SMALL CAP   LOWER CASE   SWASH CAPS

DESCENDER LINE

12560 12560

FIGURES (LINING / OLDSTYLE)   AMPERSANDS

STRESS   SLOPE   X-HEIGHT

OPPOSITE: Plan of Cases adapted to Edmund Fry and Son's Great Primer Script from *Specimen of Modern Printing Types by Edmund Fry, Letter Founder to the King* (London: Edmund Fry and Son, 1828).

COUNTER BODY ASCENDER FORKED ASCENDER

a b h h p n e

FOOT EYE

DESCENDER

SWASH

e g b s h b

FLOURISH

SPINE SPINE WAIST BOWL

n R K r Q a

SHOULDER LEG KNEE ARM TAIL TAIL

y g g g e i G

TONGUE DOT JAW

TAIL LOOP LINK EAR

G G t C P A

CHIN BEARD TRIANGLE SPUR BRACKET (FILLET) APEX

M A f T K r

VERTEX CROSSBAR CROSS STROKE JUNCTURE CROTCH

LIGATURES: HISTORICAL   FUNCTIONAL   QUAINT   SILLY

NESTED LETTER

BOWED **R**

LONG **S**   ESZETT   EXIT & ENTRY STROKES   JOINS   REVERSE WEIGHT   CHAMFER

STENCIL   SPUR   ORNAMENT   LOGOTYPE

HAIRLINE SERIF   BRACKETED SERIF   CUPPED SERIF   WEDGE SERIF

SLAB SERIF   BRACKETED SLAB SERIF   BIFURCATED SERIF   FLARED SERIF   TAPERED STROKE   SANS SERIF

BEAK SERIF   HAIRLINE SERIF   SLAB SERIF   CALLIGRAPHIC TERMINAL   LOBE TERMINAL   BALL TERMINAL

IXTVS PP

PAVPERV

OMMODIT

MVLIERV

XTRVI FEC

M·D·LXXXVI

PONT·IIII

Inscriptional Letters

Letters carved into a surface—usually stone but also wood or metal—are described as being inscriptional. (Some type classification schemes call them glyphic.) This chapter looks at six typefaces whose inspiration comes from a diverse array of inscriptions ranging in time from Ancient Rome to the Renaissance. In judging these typefaces it should be kept in mind that two aspects of inscriptional letters, scale and depth, are lost in the transformation from stone or wood to print.

The letters comprising the inscription at the base of Trajan's Column in Rome (114 AD) are the archetype of the Roman alphabet for many. Known as *Capitalis Monumentalis* or Imperial Roman capitals, they disappeared with the fall of the Roman Empire, only to be rediscovered and revived several times in the centuries since. During the Romanesque era (c. 1000–c. 1150) they were mixed with uncial letters, but in the Renaissance sculptors, painters, and scribes strived to replicate their purity of form, free of medieval influences. The first attempts by florentine sculptors of the early Quattrocento resulted in modulated sans serif letters, but by the middle of the 15th century, artists and scribes in Padua and Venice had succeeded in closely approximating the seriffed majesty of the *Capitalis Monumentalis* in manuscripts, paintings, and frescoes. Their efforts influenced the capitals of the first Roman typefaces that emerged in Venice in the 1470s.

The first typeface modeled explicitly on inscriptional letters was the Caractéres Augustaux commissioned by Lyonnaise printer Louis Perrin (1799–1865) and cut by Francisque Rey. It was used to print *Inscriptions Antiques de Lyon* by Alphonse de Boissieu (1846). A lowercase was added in 1855. (Louize [2014] by Alice Savoie is a digital version.) Frederic W. Goudy (1865–1947) designed several typefaces directly inspired by specific inscriptions: Forum (1911), Hadriano (1918) and Trajan (1930). But with the exception of Sistina (1951) by Hermann Zapf (1918–2015), most other inscriptional typefaces of the pre-digital era—such as Columna (1955) by Max Caflisch (1916–2004)—have been modern interpretations rather than revivals.

Because inscriptions have historically been composed in all capital letters, most typefaces inspired by them have been titling types. However, three of the typefaces in this chapter have a lowercase as well.

OPPOSITE: Detail of plate 9 from *Varie inscrittioni del santiss. S. N. Sisto V pont. max.* by Luca Horfei (Rome: all'insegna del Lupo in Parione, 1589). Horfei's capitals were the inspiration for Horfei (LetterPerfect, 1996) by Garrett Boge.

TRAJAN

The letters of the inscription at the base of Trajan's Column in Rome, long considered the epitome of classical Roman capitals, were the inspiration for Adobe Trajan (1989) by Carol Twombly (b. 1959). The principal source for her design was a photocopy of a rubbing of the inscription by Father E. M. Catich, author of *Letters Redrawn from the Trajan Inscription in Rome* (1961) and *The Origin of the Serif* (1968). However, there was still much for Twombly to select, interpret and invent to turn the inscription into a typeface. With the exception of **H**, the inscription includes all of the twenty letters of the alphabet used by the Romans. She had to create the missing letters plus Arabic figures, punctuation, and currency symbols. Adobe Trajan was originally issued with Lithos and Charlemagne as part of The Modern Ancients trio of display typefaces.

In 2012, Adobe Trajan was redesigned and extended by Robert Slimbach (b. 1956). It was renamed Adobe Trajan Pro 3. Several alternate letters and ligatures were added to the glyph palette; Greek and Cyrillic characters were created; and the family was enlarged to include Extra Light, Light, Regular, Semibold, Bold, and Black. Slimbach also designed from scratch a matching sans serif family called Adobe Trajan Sans Pro. Both Adobe Trajan Pro 3 and Adobe Trajan Sans Pro are titling faces.

Detail of the inscription at the base of Trajan's Column in Rome. Photograph by Richard Kindersley, 1997.

Adobe Trajan Pro3 | Carol Twombly (Adobe, 1989) – Robert Slimbach (Adobe, 2012)

ABCDEFGHIJKLMNOPQQRST
UVWXYYZ&&&NNTT
1234567890{[(.,;:!?*)]}¶

Adobe Trajan Sans Pro | Robert Slimbach (Adobe, 2012)

ABCDEFGHIJKLMNOPQQRSTU
VWXYYZ&&&NNTT
1234567890{[(.,;:!?*)]}¶

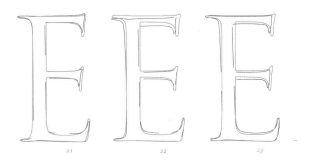

COMPARISON (ABOVE): Adobe Trajan Pro 3 vs. Adobe Trajan Sans Pro.
COMPARISON (BELOW): Three of 21 different **E**s in the Trajan inscription (in light blue) superimposed on **E** from Adobe Trajan Pro (in black).

ROMANESQUE

Alverata by Gerard Unger (b. 1942) is a contemporary interpretation of Romanesque capitals that grew out of his dissertation on the subject. It is distilled from a study of numerous Romanesque inscriptions in Italy, France, and the Netherlands. Romanesque capitals, such as those illustrated here from an early 12th century inscription on the facade of the cathedral in Pisa, are notable for their wild variety of forms (classical, uncial, square and pointed). They are also frequently ligatured and nested. They have low stroke contrast and stubby bracketed serifs.

Unger applied his own distinctive aesthetic—developed over forty years in typefaces from Demos and Praxis to Swift and Gulliver—to the Romanesque forms to create Alverata's three variants (Regular, Informal and Irregular). He also invented lowercase companions, figures and punctuation for each. Unger's letters are not as wild as his Romanesque models, allowing Alverata to be used broadly rather than relegated to designs requiring historical allusiveness. The Romanesque flavor is primarily evident in the Informal and Irregular versions (e.g., **A** with a forked bar and uncial **E**), both of which can be mixed with the Regular version or each other to achieve additional levels of strangeness.

Detail of a Romanesque inscription (1063) on the facade of the cathedral in Pisa commemorating a naval victory against the Saracens near Palermo. Photograph by Paul Shaw, 2016.

Alverata Regular, Informal, and Irregular | Gerard Unger (TypeTogether, 2014)

AAABBCDEEEFFGGHIJKKLMNNOO
PPQQRRSSTUUVVWWXXYYZZ&
ABCDEFGHIJKLMNOPQRSTUVWXYZ
aaabbbcddeeeffggghhijijkkllmm
mnnooppqqorrssttuuuvvwwxxy
yzzfffififlflffiffl{[(.,;:!?*)]}¶
1234567890123456789o

COMPARISON: **M**, **O**, **R** from Pisa cathedral inscription vs. Alverata. Below: Some distinctive letters in Alverata.

MANTEGNA

HVMANI
GENERIS
REDEMTO
RI

Mantinia | Matthew Carter (Carter & Cone, 1993)

ABCDEFGHIIJKLLMNOPQQR
RSTTTUVWXYYYZ&&
CTÆLAMBMDÆMPEHTTTUTW
TYUPCVI234567890{[(.,;:!?*)]}

Matthew Carter designed Mantinia after seeing an exhibition of the work of the Renaissance painter and printmaker Andrea Mantegna (c.1431–1506) in London in 1992. Mantegna was known for an antiquarianism that extended to the precise depiction of classical capitals in many of his works, most famously in the St. James frescoes (c.1448–c.1456) in the funeral chapel of Antonio degli Ovetari in the church of the Eremitani in Padua. But Carter was inspired by a different Mantegna work, an engraving entitled *The Entombment of Christ* (1465/1470), which includes a small monument with a short, four-line inscription: HVMANI | GENERIS | REDEMPTO | RI.

Out of these few letters Carter spun a full titling typeface, complete with alternate letters, figures, and punctuation. Encouraged by the presence of the **MP** ligature, he extended Mantinia's character set to include a wealth of ligatures, nested letters, short letters and tall letters. (Using baseline shift the hanging short letters can be positioned on the baseline to create additional nesting pairs.)

The capitals of Mantinia (Mantegna's name in Latin) are robust with a low stem width-to-height proportion and strongly bracketed serifs. Carter made them this way so that they could work together with his Galliard typeface (ITC, 1978 and Carter & Cone, 1993) based on the types of the 16th-century French punchcutter Robert Granjon (1513–1590). Although Mantinia successfully harmonizes with Galliard, it also works admirably on its own as a display typeface.

OPPOSITE: Detail of *The Entombment of Christ* engraved by Andrea Mantegna (1465/1470).
ABOVE: Some distinctive letters in Mantinia.

ARRIGHI

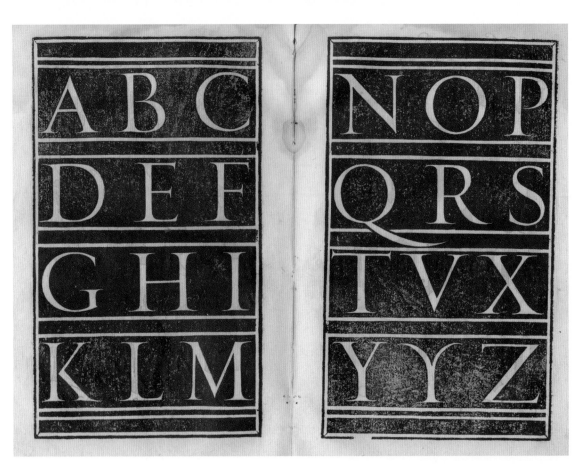

The Renaissance calligrapher Ludovico Vicentino degli Arrighi (c. 1480–1527), well-known as the author of *La Operina* (1522), the first writing manual, has long been celebrated for his chancery italic hand. However, Requiem by Jonathan Hoefler (b. 1970) is derived instead from a set of Roman capitals designed by Arrighi and cut into wood by Eustachio Celebrino da Udine that appear in his second book titled *Essemplare di Piu Sorti Lettere* (1524). Hoefler has filled in the alphabet and added swash alternates for **K, N, Q, R** and **T**. The elegant palmate **Y** comes from the Greek letter ypsilon.

The capitals of Requiem Display are supplemented with a set of beautiful cartouches inspired by the work of other Renaissance writing masters, most notably Giovanni Battista Palatino (c. 1515–c. 1575). (The ribbon ends, though, were influenced by the work of Hermann Zapf.) The width of the cartouches can be adjusted with the addition of cameo versions of the capitals.

Alongside Requiem Display and Requiem Fine, there is also Requiem Text. To the Arrighi-inspired capitals Hoefler added a lowercase in the Venetian Oldstyle manner (but with the lightness of Centaur) and an italic of his own invention as well as the requisite figures, punctuation and symbols of a modern glyph set. Thus, Requiem can be used as a text face.

Alphabet of Roman capitals from *Il modo da imparare di scriuere littera Cancellarescha* by Ludovico Vicentino degli Arrighi (Venice, 1523–1525).

Requiem Display | Ludovico Vicentino degli Arrighi (1524) – Jonathan Hoefler (Hoefler Type Foundry, 1992)

ABCDEFGHIJKKLMNNOPQQRR
STTUVWXYYZ&ABCDEFGHIJKKLM
NNOPQQRRSTTUVWXYYZabcdefghijkl
mnpqrstuvwxyzčtfbfffhfifjfkflffbffhffiffj
ffkfflſtı1234567890{[(.,;:!?ˣ⋆)]}◖❧❦

COMPARISON: **B**, **R**, **Y** from the alphabet by Arrighi vs. Requiem.

DELLA ROBBIA

A sans serif capital marked by thick/thin contrast and wedge-shaped stroke endings first appeared in Florentine sculpture in the statue of *St. John the Baptist* (1412–1416) in Orsanmichele by Lorenzo Ghiberti (1378–1455). Variations of this style of letterform, often with tapered instead of wedge-shaped stroke endings, subsequently dominated the work of other Florentine artists such as Donatello, Michelozzo, and Brunelleschi before spreading throughout Tuscany and other parts of Italy from Naples north to Milan and Venice.

One of the purest interpretations of this Florentine Sans, as Nicolete Gray dubbed it, can be found on the *Cantoria* (1437) designed by Luca della Robbia (1400–1482), originally in the Duomo in Florence but now in the Museo del Duomo. Its three-line inscription was the principal model for Donatello by Paul Shaw (b. 1954). Some letters, as well as those of Donatello Alternativo, were taken from other examples of the Florentine Sans in Santa Trinità, S.anta Croce and Santissima Annunziata in Florence. Donatello and Donatello Alternativo were issued as part of The Florentine Set with Ghiberti and Beata, two other interpretations of the Florentine Sans. Garrett Boge (b. 1951) was the designer of the lighter Beata and a co-designer with Shaw of the heavier Ghiberti. He handled the digitization for the entire set.

Compare Donatello and Donatello Alternativo to Hermann Zapf's Optima (p. 231), which was also inspired by examples of the Florentine Sans.

Detail of the *Cantoria* of Luca della Robbia (1437) originally in the Duomo in Florence. Photograph by Paul Shaw, 2007.

Donatello and Donatello Alternativo | Luca della Robbia (1437) – Paul Shaw with Garrett Boge
(LetterPerfect, 1997)

ABCDEFGHIJKLMNOPQRSTUVWXYZ&
ABCDEFGHIJKLMNOPQRSTUVWX
XYZ1234567890{[(.,;:!?*)]}¶

Beata | Bernardo Rossellino (1451) – Garrett Boge with Paul Shaw (LetterPerfect. 1997)

ABCDEFGHIJKLMNOPQRSTUVWXYZ&
1234567890{[(.,;:!?*)]}¶

Ghiberti | Lorenzo Ghiberti (1425–1452) – Paul Shaw and Garrett Boge (LetterPerfect, 1997)

ABCDEFGHIJKLMNOPQRSTUV
WXYZ&1234567890{[(.,;:!?*)]}¶

COMPARISON: **M, N, R** from the *Cantoria* inscription (1437) vs. Donatello.

SANTA CROCE

On October 3, 1950 Hermann Zapf visited Santa Croce in Florence as part of a broader trip to Italy. There he was particularly struck by the Florentine Sans lettering on a number of floor tombs, especially that of Berto di Lionardo Berti (d. 1430). The letters he sketched that day, including some on the front and back of a thousand-lire note he resorted to when he ran out of paper, were the seeds of Optima (1958), a humanist sans serif notable for the subtle entasis of its strokes. (For more on Optima Nova as a revival/redesign of the original foundry type from D. Stempel see pp. 230–231.)

A titling font was added to the Optima family in 2002 when it was redesigned by Zapf with the assistance of Akira Kobayashi (b. 1960). The capitals of Optima Nova Titling are softer in appearance than those of regular Optima Nova. The corners of stroke endings are gently rounded while the corners of counters and stroke junctures are "filled-in." The character set includes alternates, tall letters, nested letters and ligatures. This soft feature and these additional characters have no basis in Florentine Sans inscriptions, but instead hark back to 1959 lettering designed by Zapf for a Petrarch quotation to be cast in metal (see p. 226).

TOP: Sketches by Hermann Zapf on the back of a thousand-lire note (1950).
ABOVE RIGHT: Detail of the inscription on the floor tomb (c. 1453) of Spinello di Bonsignori de' Spinelli (d. 1381) in Santa Croce, Florence. Photograph by Massimo Pesce, 2015.

Optima Nova Titling | Hermann Zapf with Akira Kobayashi (Linotype, 2002)

ABCDEEFGHIJKLMNOPQQRSTTU
UVWXYZ&AADEFTHEHRKALAMENE
NNOOOOQUSTTETHTITTCHLILLRESAVE
1234567890{[(.,;:!?*)]}¶

COMPARISON (ABOVE): **E**, **N**, **R** from Spinelli tomb vs. Optima Nova Titling; RIGHT: **R** from Optima Nova Regular.
BELOW: Some distinctive characters from Optima Nova Titling.

And k
here k
That
ABC.

Blackletter

Blackletter describes the dark, angular scripts of the Middle Ages that dominated European manuscripts between the Carolingian era and the Renaissance. There are four major varieties of blackletter: textura, rotunda, bâtarde, and fraktur. Textura was a northern European script, while rotunda was primarily found in Italy and Spain; bâtarde, commonly used for books of hours, was predominantly French, Burgundian, and Flemish; and fraktur, although invented in southern Germany, was prevalent in countries with German-speaking populations. All served as models for typefaces in the first century of printing before eventually being superseded by roman type in most of Europe. (The exception was Germany, where blackletter remained the dominant style of type until the end of World War II.)

The first typeface in the West, the B42 type of Johannes Gutenberg (c. 1398–1468), was a textura. Textura—often called Old English in the Anglo-American world—has been the most important style of blackletter ever since, with the widest distribution and the greatest longevity. Even after roman type overtook blackletter in popularity, textura lingered on in the worlds of the church, the university, and journalism. Long identified with beer advertising and packaging, in the 20th century it also became associated with punk, heavy metal and hiphop music. It is a staple lettering style for tattoos.

Textura is the darkest of all blackletters. The lowercase letters are angular and condensed with a tall x-height and feet (small diamond-shaped strokes) instead of serifs. Curves are broken into verticals and diagonals. Ascenders are often forked at the top. In contrast, the capitals, modeled on a mix of roman and uncial forms, are broader, with some having generous curves. They are usually heavily ornamented with hairlines or tendrils paralleling strokes or bridging counters, diamonds filling negative spaces, and hackles sprouting from stems. Oftentimes, stems are doubled.

This chapter includes three revivals of texturas, two ancient and one modern.

OPPOSITE: Detail of Four Lines Pica Black, No. 3 from *Specimen of Printing Types by Caslon & Livermore, Letter-Founders, Chiswell Street, London* (London: Bensley, Printer, 1825).

Gutenberg

The *Biblia Latina* printed by Johannes Gutenberg around 1455 is set in a textura typeface modeled on the calligraphy of contemporaneous German manuscripts. The B42 typeface (so-called because there are forty-two lines on a page of the Bible) has 299 characters in its font. The large character set is the result of Gutenberg's desire to match the quality of letterspacing, wordspacing and justification found in a manuscript. To achieve that end, the same strategies used by scribes—narrow alternate letters, ligatures, and letters with abbreviations—were employed. Whether the B42 type was the work of Gutenberg or of his assistant Peter Schoeffer (1425–1503), an accomplished calligrapher and the father of the punchcutter Peter Schoeffer II (c. 1475–1547), is still under debate.

Gutenberg B by José Alberto Mauricio is an attempt to recreate the complete B42 character set, based on Alois Ruppel's chart in the 1925 *Gutenberg Festschrft*. Note especially the lowercase letters (e.g., **n**) missing their left entry stroke in order to allow tighter kerning; the multiple-letter ligatures (e.g., **chas**); the angled and upright forms of **d**; the bowed form of **r**; and the long **s** and curvy raised terminal **s** along with the familiar short **s**. To make the typeface functional today Mauricio has created missing letters (e.g., **k** and **w**), Arabic figures and modern punctuation. He has also added a group of quaint **s** ligatures which are not found in the B42 font.

A more "modern" interpretation of Gutenberg's B42 typeface that ignores the alternate letters, ligatures, and abbreviations is Zur Laden (1997) by Bo Berndal (b. 1924).

Detail of a leaf from II Maccabees, 1–2, *Biblia Latina* printed by Johannes Gutenberg (1455).

Gutenberg B | Johannes Gutenberg (1455) – José Alberto Mauricio (Alter Littera, 2012)

ᚹᚨᛒᛟᛚᛚᛞᛖᛖᚠᚠᚠᚠᚷᚷᚺᛁᛁᛁᚲᛁᛗᚨᛟᛈᛟᚱᚱ
ᛋᛏᚢᚤᛗᛁᚹᛉᛦᛉᛉ...

(decorative blackletter alphabet and ligature specimen — letterforms as shown)

COMPARISON: *Biblia Latina* vs. Alter Littera Gutenberg B.

Van den Keere

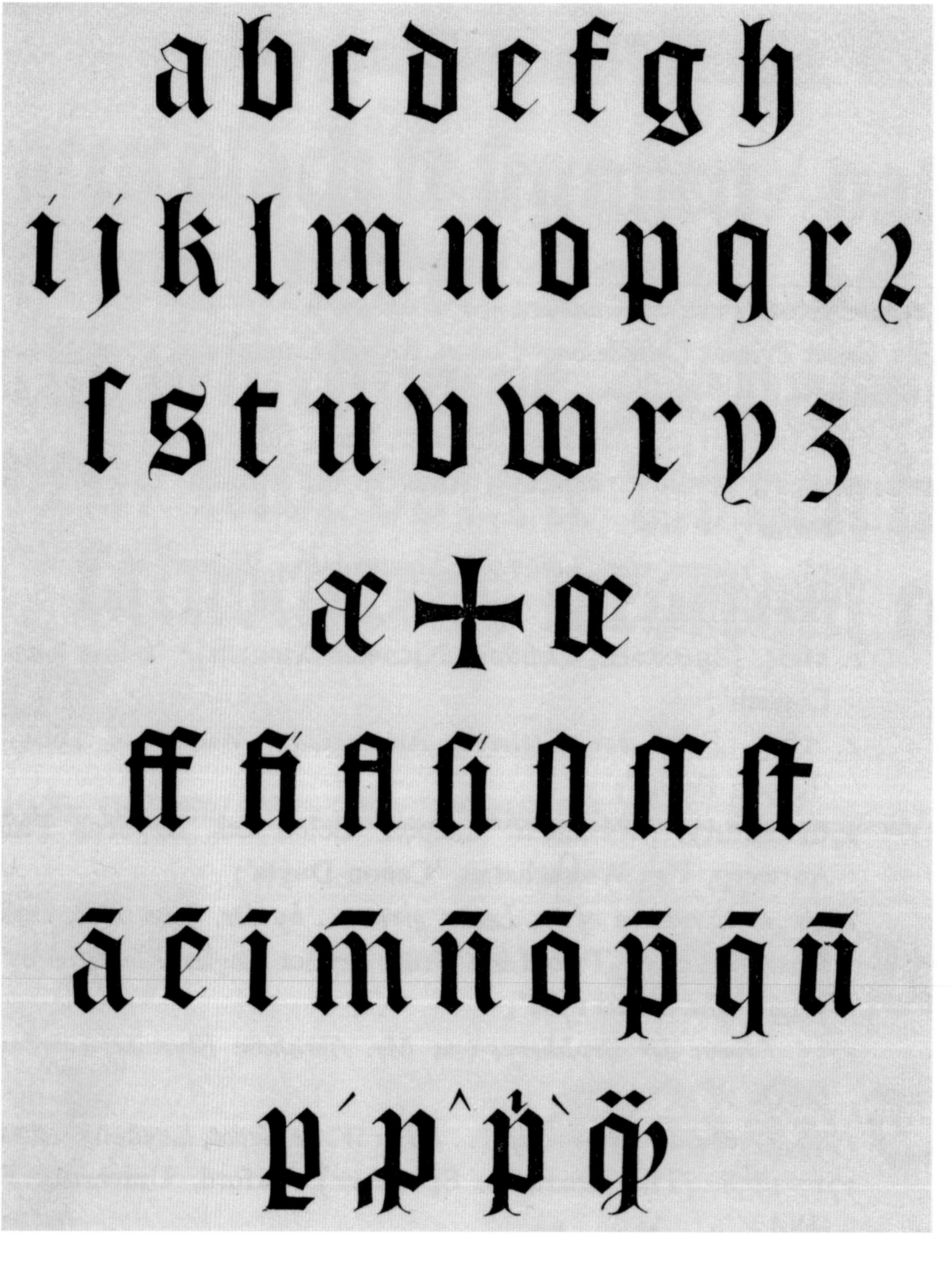

a b c d e f g h

i j k l m n o p q r z

ſ s t u v w x y z

x ✠ œ

ff ſh ſk ſi ſl ſſ ſt

ã ẽ ĩ m̃ ñ õ p̃ q̃ ũ

ẏ ṕ p̂ p̈

Flamande with Flamande Archaic | Hendrik Van den Keere 2-line Canon Textura (1570) and Paragon Textura (1585) – Matthew Carter (Carter & Cone, 1996)

ABCDDEFGHIJKLMNOPQRS
TUVWXYZ+1234567890(.,;:!)¶
abcdefghijklmnopqqrrzsstuvwxyz
kelochckladedffffiffffiflkelpijcorpraldshli
flststtztatithtz

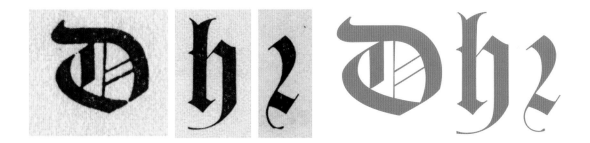

A prominent link in the evolution of Old English from its origins in the 1498 textura of the Parisian printer Simon Vostre (active 1488–1518) to its familiar form in the 1821 black letter of W. Caslon Jr. (1781–1869) are the texturas of the 16th-century Flemish punchcutter Hendrik van den Keere (c. 1541–1580). Two of them, the 2-line Canon Textura (1571) and the Paragon Textura (1585), are the sources for Flamande by Matthew Carter. Punches for both types survive at the Plantin-Moretus Museum in Antwerp, but the capitals for the larger type are missing. They are reproduced in H. D. L. Vervliet's *Sixteenth-Century Printing Types of the Low Countries* (1967).

Carter's Flamande is a very faithful rendition of Van den Keere's designs, complete with the archaic characters such as long **s**, bowed **r** and various abbreviations. The extensive set of ligatures has been extrapolated from various books printed in textura. The only character that has been modernized is capital **I**. Arabic figures and a limited set of modern punctuation marks have been added to make the typeface usable today.

OPPOSITE: 2-line Canon Textura (1570) by Henrik van den Keere, cast in matrices at the Plantin-Moretus Museum (MA 4).
COMPARISON (ABOVE): **D** from Paragon Textura; **h**, bowed **r** from 2-line Canon Textura with Flamande and Flamande Archaic.

Koch

Rudolf Koch (1876–1934) was a calligrapher, type designer and illustrator. He worked for the Gebr. Klingspor foundry and and through the Offenbacher Werkstatt designed calligraphic work in a wide range of media from manuscripts and woodcuts to tapestries. Koch, a devoted exponent of blackletter, was the greatest designer of blackletter types in the 20th century. His masterpiece was Wilhelm Klingspor Schrift (Gebr. Klingspor, 1926), named in memory of Wilhelm Klingspor, who died in 1925. It is a textura that combines both power and grace. Its character set includes a second set of narrower capitals, several lowercase alternate letters, a few swash letters for justification and decoration, and a large number of ligatures.

In the 1980s Linotype, the heir to the Klingspor foundry and owner of the rights to Wilhelm Klingspor Schrift, had issued (in conjunction with Adobe) a bastardized PostScript version based on the decorative display sizes. It lacked the second set of capitals, the alternate characters and ligatures. Furthermore, the **A**, **k** and **x** had been redrawn to make them more familiar to modern users. The Alter Littera version of Wilhelm Klingspor Schrift, designed by José Alberto Mauricio, has brought back Koch's complete character set, but the lack of modern alternates for the difficult **A**, **k** and **x** limits the use of this beautiful typeface in the 21st century.

Paste-up proof of Wilhelm Klingspor Schrift character set (c.1925).

Wilhelm Klingspor Schrift | Rudolf Koch (Gebr. Klingspor, 1925) – José Alberto Mauricio (Alter Littera, 2013)

COMPARISON: Wide and narrow O, es ligature from proof of Wilhelm Klingspor Schrift; wide O from foundry type Wilhelm Klingspor Schrift vs. wide and narrow O, es ligature from Alter Littera Wilhelm Klingspor Schrift. Note the simplification of the decorative elements.

VSEBIVM Pamphili de euangelica præparatione
latinum ex græco beatissime pater iussu tuo effeci.
Nam quom eum uirum tum eloquétia: tū multaꝛ
rerum peritia: et īgenii mirabili flumine ex his quæ
iam traducta sunt præstātissimum sanctitas tua iu-
dicet: atꝗ ideo quæcūꝗ apud græcos ipsius opera
extét latina facere īstituerit: euangelicā præpationé
quæ in urbe forte reperta est: primum aggressi tra-
duximus. Quo quidem in libro quasi quodam in speculo uariam atꝗ
multiplicem doctrinā illius uiri licet admirari. Cuncta enim quæ ante
ipsū facta īuentaꝗ fuerunt quæ tamen græce scripta tūc inuenirétur:
multo certius atque distinctius ipsis etiam auctoribus qui scripserunt
percepisse mihi uidetur. Ista quom constet nihil fere præclarum unꝗ
gestum fuisse quod illis temporibus græce scriptum non extaret: nihil
in rebus magnis naturaꝗ abditis quod a philosophis non esset expli-
catum: omnia ille tum memoriæ tenacitate: tū métis pcepit acumine:
ac ut apes solent singulis insidere floribus: indeꝗ quod ad rem suam
conducit colligere: nó aliter ille undiꝗ certiora uerisimilioraue deligés
mirabilem sibi atꝗ inauditū scientiæ cumulum confecit: multiplices
uariasꝗ philosophorum sectas nó ignorauit: infinitos pene gentium
omnium religionis errores tenuit: orbis terrarum historiam serie sua
dispositam solus cognouit & cæteris tradidit. Nam quom non esset
nescius gestaꝛ rerum historiam titubare sāctissime pater nisi distincta
téporibus pateat. Quippe quom natura téporis faciat ut quæ ī tépore
fuerunt nisi quando fuerūt scias: nec fuisse qdem ꝓpter confusionem
uideantur: eo ingenio: studio: industria huic incubuit rei: ut omnium
scriptorum peritiam in unum congestam facile su pauerit: distictiusꝗ
cuncta ipsis suis ut diximus cognouerit auctoribus. Conferendo enim
inter se singulos: ueritatem quæ ab omnibus simul emergebat: nec ab
ullo exprimebatur: consecutus est. Quæ omnia ab aliis quæ scripsit &
ab hoc opere perspicere licet. Quod ille ideo suscepit: quoniam quom
apud gentiū præclaros philosophia uiros nobilissimus esset: ac priscā
paternamꝗ deorū religionem catholicæ ueritatis amore cótempserit:
partim accusātibus suum propositum respondere: partim nostra pro
uiribus suis uoluit cófirmare. Itaꝗ ī duas uniuersum partis negotium
partitus est: quarum primam quæ nunc traducta nobis est: qua illis

Venetian Oldstyle and Aldine Types

The first printers in Italy were Konrad Sweynheym (d. 1477) and Arnold Pannartz (d. 1476), two German printers invited to set up a press in 1465 at the Benedictine monastery in Subiaco. Their typeface was a gotico-antiqua, a hybrid of textura and roman forms. The first roman type, though still with gothic influences (such as **h** with curled leg), appeared in a Cicero printed by Johannes da Spira (d. 1470) in Venice in 1469. A year later, Nicolas Jenson (c. 1420–1480), a French printer working in Venice issued a Eusebius in a typeface that is generally acclaimed to be the first pure roman. His type and others used by printers in Venice such as Erhard Ratdolt (1442–1528) in the 1470s and 1480s are classed as Venetian Oldstyle.

Venetian Oldstyle types were modeled after contemporary humanist manuscripts—though no specific ones have yet been identified—written in littera antica, a script combining pen-made imitations of classical Roman capitals with small letters derived from the Carolingian minuscule. The letters tend to be heavy with low stroke contrast, a diagonal bias to curves, and blunt bracketed serifs. The capitals are wide with generous bowls and the same height as ascenders. In the lowercase, the bowl of **a** is small, the thin stroke of **e** is angled upward and extends beyond the upper curve, the tail of **y** is straight, and **z** has horizontals heavier than the diagonal. There were no italic types.

In the 1490s Francesco Griffo (1450–c. 1518) cut types for Aldus Manutius (1449–1515) that were significantly lighter, crisper and more refined than those of Jenson et al. The serifs were sharper, and the capitals were narrower and shorter. Griffo (who was also known as Francesco da Bologna) was the first to cut an italic typeface, though the capitals were roman. It was used by Aldus to print small portable books intended for scholars and students.

This chapter focuses on three interpretations of Jenson's roman and one of Griffo's roman.

OPPOSITE: *De evangelica praeparatione* by Eusebius of Caesarea (tr. Georgius Trapezuntius). Printed by Nicolas Jenson (Venice, 1470).

Jenson

Nicolas Jenson was a French-born printer/punchcutter who worked in Venice from 1470 until his death. The type used in his first book, an edition of Eusebius (1470), has been long been considered the first roman face free of gothic elements. Since the 1890s it has been the basis for innumerable typefaces (see pp. 164–167), including several digital interpretations. The most accurate is Adobe Jenson by Robert Slimbach. It captures the robust weight of Jenson's type and its character set has only been minimally modernized with the option of **M** without double head serifs, **Q** with a shorter tail, narrower **Z**, and ahistorical ligatures such as **Th**. Adobe Jenson was originally issued as a Multiple Master typeface with optical sizes.

Adobe Jenson was preceded by Abrams Venetian by lettering artist George Abrams (1919–2001) and ITC Legacy Serif by graphic designer Ron Arnholm (b. 1939), two personal interpretations of Jenson's typeface adapted to modern tastes. Both have dispensed with the distinctive double head serifs on **M**, narrowed letters **H** and **Z**, and reduced the size of the bowl of **P**. They have also sharpened the beak serifs in the lowercase. Abrams and Arnholm differ most notably in their treatment of **W**, **J** (letters not used by Jenson), and **y**. ITC Legacy Serif has a taller x-height than either Adobe Jenson or Abrams Venetian.

Abrams Venetian, digitized by Charles Nix (b. 1967), was initially designed for the sole use of the Danish government, but it has since been made commercially available. ITC Legacy Serif has two companions, ITC Legacy Sans (1992) and ITC Legacy Square Serif (2009), designed by Arnholm. The latter retains Jenson's structure but has unbracketed serifs that give it a contemporary feel.

Detail of f.1 from *De evangelica praeparatione* by Eusebius of Caesarea. Printed by Nicolas Jenson (Venice, 1470).

Adobe Jenson Pro Subhead | Nicolas Jenson (1470) – Robert Slimbach (Adobe, 1996)

ABCDEFGHIJKLMMNOPQQRSTU
VWXYZZ&ABCDEFGHIJKLMNOPQRSTU
vwxyz&abcdefghijklmnopqqrsftuvwxyz
Thctfffifjflffifjfflspstshfisflsfst1234567890
1234567890{[(.,;:!?*)]}❦✿✤✦

Abrams Venetian | Nicolas Jenson (1470) – George Abrams with Charles Nix (Expert Alphabets, 1987)

ABCDEFGHIJKLMNOPQRSTUVW
XYZ&ABCDEFGHIJKLMNOPQRSTUVW
xyzabcdefghijklmnopqrrstuvwxyz
ctstfifl12345678901234567890{[(.,;:!?*)]}¶

M M M M

COMPARISON: Adobe Jenson Pro (two leftmost letters) | Abrams Venetian | ITC Legacy Serif Pro.

G G G

a a a

g g g

g

ITC Legacy Serif Pro Book | Nicolas Jenson (1470) – Ron Arnholm (ITC, 1992)

ABCDEFGHIJKLMNOPQRSTUVW
XYZ&ABCDEFGHIJKLMNOPQRSTUVWX
yz&abcdefghijklmnopqrstuvwxyz
fffiflffifflı234567890ı234567890
{[(.,;:!?*)]}¶

ITC Legacy Square Serif Pro Book | Nicolas Jenson (1470) – Ron Arnholm (ITC, 2009)

ABCDEFGHIJKLMNOPQRSTUVW
XYZ&ABCDEFGHIJKLMNOPQRSTUVWX
yz&abcdefghijklmnopqrstuvwxyz
fffiflffifflı234567890ı234567890
{[(.,;:!?*)]}¶

COMPARISON: ITC Legacy Serif Pro | ITC Legacy Square Serif Pro | ITC Legacy Sans Pro.

Griffo

licet esse tam disertis: Qui n
hanc linguarum uarietate
n est Romanis lingua, qua
. Aliter Florentini loquun
nsibus lingua, & pronuntia
s.alius Bergomatibus sern

Francesco Griffo is the first professional punchcutter who was not also a printer for whom we have reliable documentation. He cut punches for Pietro Maufer, the brothers Giovanni and Gregorio De Gregori, Aldus Manutius and Gershom Soncino. His types for Aldus, including a Greek, two of the romans and the first italic, have all been influential. The second roman, used in the celebrated *Hypnerotomachia Poliphilii* (1499), became the basis for Poliphilus (Monotype Corporation, 1922) while the first, employed in *De Aetna* by Pietro Bembo (1496), was used as the model for Bembo (Monotype Corporation, 1929). Griffo's romans, considered to be lighter, crisper and more refined than Jenson's roman, inspired the types of Claude Garamont (see pp. 52–55).

Named after a Greek club founded by Aldus, Neacademia by Sergei Egerov (b. 1963) is the most recent digital interpretation of Griffo's romans that is commercially available. (Both Yale by Matthew Carter for Yale University [2004] and Grolier by Jerry Kelly for The Grolier Club [2015] are proprietary designs.) Unlike Poliphilus or Bembo, it is not based on the types of a single book. Thus it contains multiple versions of many lowercase letters that differ only subtly from each other, reflecting the changing appearance of Griffo's romans in the 1490s. Optimal spacing of the font requires that contextual alternates be turned on in InDesign. In addition, Neacademia comes in four optical sizes (subtext, text, subhead and display).

Detail of f.2 from *Thesaurus Cornucopiae et Horti Adonidis* edited by Aldus Manutius and Urbanus Bolzanius (Venice: Aldus Manutius, 1496).

Neacademia Text | Francesco Griffo (Aldus Manutius, 1495) – Sergei Egerov (Rosetta, 2012)

ABCDEFGHIJKLMNOPQRSTU
VWXYZ& ABCDEFGHIJKLMNO
PQRSTUVWXYZ&aabbcdeeeef
ggghiijkllmmnnooooppqrrsttuuvv
wxyyzzchckctfbfffhfifjfkflstffbfhffi
ffjffkffl{[(.,;:!?*)]} ☾ ❧
1234567890I234567890I234567890

COMPARISON: **b**s from Griffo's roman vs. Neacademia.

lis, quàm in cæteris omnibus pro[c]

e Romana cultum faciant. Qua

~ sacras linguas, Hebraicam, G[

umani ingenij artes, Musicen, .[

[a]ctenus. quæ si hoc uno Catholi[

Atque huius pietatis exemplo, [

~ testimonia, hæc sacra Biblia[

mmendatum vobis semper, sem[

sancto negotio mecum suos labo[

ti appendicem, hoc est viduæ ill[

uid illa ad Catholicæ pietatis [a[

nque religione ac pietate calent[

tissimo animo, & magno ac pro[

French Oldstyle Types

Prior to the 1520s French printing was done almost exclusively in gothic types. The shift to roman types was led by Geofroy Tory (1480–1533), a true Renaissance man—poet, translator, scholar, calligrapher, illustrator, engraver, printer, publisher, bookseller, and orthographic reformer—and the Parisian printer Simon de Colines (1480–1546) who began his career as the foreman in the printing office of Henri Estienne the Elder (1470–1520). In 1520 Colines married Estienne's widow and ran the press until 1526 when his stepson Robert Estienne (1503–1559) became old enough to take over. Colines then established his own print shop.

The books printed by Colines in the 1520s employed floriated criblè initials and borders designed by Tory and roman types he had cut himself in imitation of Italian models. The combination, seen in the *Grandes Heures de Simon de Colines* (1525), established a new, lighter style of French printing. In 1528 Colines was the first printer to use mated roman and italic types together in a single book. He cut italics in the manner of both Griffo and Arrighi.

Unlike Colines, Robert Estienne did not cut his own types but commissioned them from several punchcutters, among them Claude Garamont (c. 1510–1561), who made a trade by selling strikes from his punches. Garamont's types, in particular his romans, which first appear in use around 1530, helped to establish the reputation of Estienne, Michel de Vascosan (c. 1500–1576), Jacques Kerver (d. 1583), Jean de Tournes (1504–1564), and other French printers. They were commonly paired with the italics of Robert Granjon. Both were used widely by printers outside of France for over two hundred years.

Although best remembered today, Garamont and Granjon were not the only punchcutters who contributed to making the 16th century the Golden Age of French printing. Others of importance were Colines, Antoine Augereau (c. 1485–1534), the still-unidentified Maître Constantin, François Guyot (d. 1570), and Pierre Haultin (c. 1510–1587). Augereau, notorious for having been burnt at the stake for contributing types to a heretical work, was one of the first French punchcutters to model his types on those of Griffo—a taste he passed on to his apprentice Garamont. Haultin was unrivaled as a cutter of small types.

OPPOSITE: Detail of a page from *Biblia Sacra Hebraica, Chaldaice, Graece, & Latine...* (Polyglot Bible) edited by Benedictus Arias Montanus (Antwerp: Christophe Plantin, 1469–1472), vol. 1. The italic typeface is by Robert Granjon.

Most of these punchcutters supplied types to the Flemish printer Christophe Plantin (1514–1589), several of which were used in the famous Polyglot Bible (1569–1573). Much of what we know about their types comes from the *Index sive Specimen Characterum Christophori Plantini* issued in 1567 which contains forty-one varieties of letter: seven Hebrews, six Greeks, twelve romans, ten italics, three scripts and three gothics. Another key document is the specimen sheet of Konrad Berner of Frankfurt, issued in 1592. It specifically identifies a number of types as the work of Claude Garamont (with his name spelled Garamond).

It was the Berner specimen, published in 1920 by the German printing historian Gustav Mori (1872–1950), that helped distinguish the types of Garamont from those of Jean Jannon (c. 1580–1658) with which they had become confused in the 19th century. Jannon's types were the basis for the many "Garamond" types issued in the 20th century, from ATF Garamond (Morris Fuller Benton, 1919) to ITC Garamond (Tony Stan, 1974). Although misnamed—and 17th century in origin—these types are commonly classed as French Oldstyle. The longevity of the types of Garamont and Granjon influenced not only French punchcutters like Jannon but others outside of France such as Christoffel van Dijck (1605/06–1669) in Amsterdam.

This chapter includes types based on the romans of Garamont, the italics of Granjon and Haultin, and romans by Van Dijck and Jannon. Given this variety of sources, it is difficult to make sweeping generalizations about French Oldstyle types. However, with the notable exception of Granjon's romans, they can be described as continuing the advances made by Griffo (hence the neologism Garaldus in the Vox classification system). They are light in color and well-proportioned. The capitals have some of the variety of width found in Imperial Roman capitals, while the ascenders and descenders are generous in length. Curved letters have diagonal bias and serifs are gently bracketed. The beak serifs on the lowercase stems are small.

Granjon's romans, the exception mentioned above, were darker and more vigorous—mannerist in the lexicon of author and typographer Robert Bringhurst (b. 1946)—than those of Garamont. They pointed the way toward the Dutch Oldstyle letter that flourished in the 17th century—the subject of the next chapter.

I

ꝃLE RECVEIL DES

INSCRIPTIONS, FIGVRES,

DEVISES, ET MASQVARADES
ordonnées en l'Hoſtel de ville à Paris
le Ieudi 17 de Feburier
1558.

APRES l'heureuſe & memorable
conqueſte faite au mois de Ianuier
ſur l'ennemi, le Roy eſtant de retour
de ſa conté d'Oye nouuellemét re-
miſe en ſon obeiſſance, delibera de
ſeiourner à Paris iuſqu'au commen-
cement de Quareſme, tant pour les plaiſirs qu'on y
pouuoit trouuer en telle ſaiſon, que pour faire grati-
fier à ſon peuple l'heur de ſes dernieres victoires, la
proſperité de ſon voiage, & la deliurance de toutes
nos premieres craintes. Durant ce tens doncques,
ne voulant en rien imiter l'inſolence des temeraires
Princes en leurs proſperes auantures, & ſe temperant
beaucoup mieus en ſon heur que n'auoit fait para-
uant ſon ennemi, ſe côtenta de mille louables paſſe-
tens aſſés acouſtumés à ſa Maieſté; en meſurant ſi

B

Garamont

eftra licencia. Mandan
erta fciencia y Real auct
s, Regentes la Cancelle
es de aquel, Aguaziles,

Most types that bear the name Garamond today are based on the roman shown in the 1621 type specimen of Jean Jannon (see pp. 66–67) not on any of the numerous types cut by Claude Garamont. The exceptions are the Garamond issued by Ollière (1914), Stempel Garamond (1924), and the two versions of Adobe Garamond designed by Robert Slimbach. The first, Adobe Garamond, was the typeface that proved to skeptical designers that digital type—with one caveat—could match the quality of design found in foundry type. That caveat was that digital type, like phototype before it, was size-independent and thus one design had to suffice for a range of uses from footnotes in books to signage and billboards. To balance these competing needs Slimbach based his Adobe Garamond on Garamont's Parangon (1557), roughly equal in size to 19 pts.

Adobe Garamond was thus a compromise, one that Slimbach made reluctantly. From the beginning, he had wanted to make optical sizes for the typeface, using Adobe's Multiple Master technology, but was unable to, due to the company's pressing need to issue the typeface. Slimbach finally got his chance after the demise of the Multiple Master technology in 2003. The result was Adobe Garamond Premier Pro with four optical sizes (caption, text, subhead and display) activated automatically by an OpenType friendly application such as InDesign.

Only a handful of digital typefaces have optical size options other than text and display. Usually, the options are based on adjustments of a single master design. However, Adobe Garamond Premier Pro is different in that each of its optical sizes is based on a different typeface by Garamont: caption on Petit-Texte (1553), text on Cicero (1552) and Gros Romain (1549), subhead on Parangon (1557), and display on Gros Canon (1549). In this way, Slimbach achieved his goal of creating a typeface that was neither rigorously faithful to its letterpress models nor homogenized.

Detail of a page from *Biblia Sacra Hebraica, Chaldaice, Graece, & Latine…* (Polyglot Bible) edited by Benedictus Arias Montanus (Antwerp: Christophe Plantin, 1469–1472), vol. 1. The roman typeface is by Claude Garamont.

Adobe Garamond Premier Pro Display | Claude Garamont (Gros Canon, 1549) – Robert Slimbach (Adobe, 2006)

ABCDEFGHIJKLMNOPQQRSTUVW
WXYZ&&&*ABCDEFGHIJKLMNOPQQR
STUVWWXYZ&abcdefghijklmnopqrstuvwxyz
adehmnrt'uz Th&fbfffh fifjfkflftft ffbffhffiffj
ffkfflfft sp st 1234567890 1234567890{[(.,:!?*)]}¶

Adobe Garamond Premier Pro Subhead | Claude Garamont (Parangon, 1557) – Robert Slimbach (Adobe, 2006)

ABCDEFGHIJKLMNOPQQRSTUV
WWXYZ&&&*ABCDEFGHIJKLMNOPQ
QRSTUVWWXYZ&abcdefghijklmnopqrstu
vwxyzadehmnrt'uz Th&fbfffh fifjfkflft
ftffbffhffiffjffkfflfft sp st{[(.,:!?*)]}¶
1234567890 1234567890

COMPARISON: Gros Romain by Garamont | Adobe Garamond Premier Pro Display | Parangon by Garamont | Adobe Garamond Pro.

G G G G

h h h h

a a a a

a a a a

OPPOSITE: Four types by Garamont: Gros Canon (1549) | Parangon (1557) | Gros Romain (1549) | Petit-Texte (1553).

Adobe Garamond Premier Pro Text | Claude Garamont (Gros Romain, 1549) – Robert Slimbach
(Adobe, 2006)

ABCDEFGHIJKLMNOPQQRSTUV
WWXYZ&&&&ABCDEFGHIJKLMNOP
QQRSTUVWWXYZ&abcdefghijklmnopqr
stuvwxyzadehmnrtuz Thctfbffffh fifj
fkfl ftft ffb ffh ffi ffj ffk ffl fft sp st
1234567890 1234567890{[(.,;:!?*)]}¶

Adobe Garamond Premier Pro Caption | Claude Garamont (Petit-Texte, 1553) – Robert Slimbach
(Adobe, 2006)

ABCDEFGHIJKLMNOPQQRSTUV
WWXYZ&&&&ABCDEFGHIJKLMNO
PQQRSTUVWWXYZ&abcdefghijklmno
pqrstuvwxyzadehmnrtuz Thctfbff
fh fi fj fk fl ft ft ffb ffh ffi ffj ffk ffl fft sp st
1234567890 1234567890{[(.,;:!?*)]}¶

gneris, c | ant Dieu. Bien | ct en la terre, que l | les Montagnes & des Chasseurs ;
apóstoli | en ce quil approu | te & la plus saine | u'on la représente toujours armé
| sil en mange : | iges n'y sont trop | eches, avec ses soixante Nymphes
| is de Foy,est pec | ux incommodité | nent compagnie par tout. Elle assi
| | ment seruir qu'en | antemens, & en cette qualité, on
| | | Lucina. Elle garda toujours la chass
| | | uffrit jamais rien qui fût contre son l
| | | D'où vint qu'elle punit l'imprudenc
| | | ir Acteon, lequel par hazard l'avoit
| | | lorsqu'elle se baignoit avec ses co

Granjon

nare, nullum vnquam ex
m Remp. fuiſſe collatum
ttentè conſiderabis, Lect
ies. Te enim tot idioma
tia, tabularum elegantia

Robert Granjon was probably the most talented punchcutter of the 16th century, surpassing even Claude Garamont. His civilités and italics, which constantly changed style during the course of his career, were his strength. Although not the first to cut inclined capitals for italics, he is credited with being the first to do so satisfactorily. In this way, Granjon's italics broke away from both of the preceding Griffo and Arrighi italics. His Parangon italic (1554) was one of the most widely used italics in Europe for two centuries, often being paired with Garamont's Parangon roman. Because of this, Robert Slimbach modeled Adobe Garamond Italic and the display and subhead optical sizes of Adobe Garamond Premier Pro Italic on it. The other two optical sizes of Adobe Garamond Premier Pro Italic were based on other Granjon italics: caption on Petit-Texte (1553),

and text on St. Augustin (1563) (with ampersands from Gros Romain [1554]).

Granjon designed four distinctly different forms of italic ampersands during his career. Kai Bernau (b.1978) synthesized the italics of Granjon's "Middle Period" (1550–1570), especially the simplicity of the more upright "droite" Cicero (1565), to create his Lyon Italic, a typeface he describes as "Neither too coldly modern, nor overly historicising."

Marian by Paul Barnes (b.1970) is an experiment in stripping a series of landmark typefaces down to the bone, to their skeletal forms. Three of its italics are copied directly from Granjon italics: Marian 1554 on the Parangon, Marian 1565 on the Cicero, and Marian 1571 on the Ascendonica. The latter is well-known as the basis for Matthew Carter's ITC Galliard Italic (1978).

Detail of a page from *Biblia Sacra Hebraica, Chaldaice, Graece, & Latine...* (Polyglot Bible) edited by Benedictus Arias Montanus (Antwerp: Christophe Plantin, 1469–1472), vol. 1. The italic typeface is by Robert Granjon.

Adobe Garamond Premier Pro Italic | Robert Granjon (Parangon Italic, 1554) – Robert Slimbach
(Adobe, 2006)

*ABCDEFGHIJKLMON PQRSTU
VWXYZ &&&&@ ABCDEFGHIJKLM
NOPQQRSTUVWXYZABCDEFGHIJKLM
NOPQQRSTUVWXYZ&abcdefghijklmnopqrst
uvwxyza d e h m n r t u vw ThThasatctet
fbfffhfifjfkflftflffbffhffifjffkfflfftisijllnt spstta
thus1234567890 1234567890{[(.,;:!?*)]}g*

COMPARISON: Swash **m**, **st** and **as** ligatures from Parangon italic by Granjon vs. Adobe Garamond Premier Pro Italic Subhead.

Adobe Garamond Premier Pro | Lyon Display Italic | Marian 1554 | Marian 1571

Lyon Display Italic | Robert Granjon (1566–1570) – Kai Bernau (OurType, 2009)

AABCDEFGHIJKLMMNOPQQQRST
UVVWWXYZÆFKKMQNRRTY
abcdefghhijjjjklmnopqrstuvvwwxyyz
&&&et)&kvvwwzThThfbfffhfhfifsfk
fkflftffbffhffhffiffiffkfflffftffk {[(.,;:!?*)]}¶
1234567890123456789o

Marian 1554 Italic | Robert Granjon (Parangon Italic, 1554) – Paul Barnes (Commercial Type, 2011)

Le Bé · Garamont

Ompée fut un des
ıs grands & des plus
ebres Generaux de
ıt l'Empire Romain.

In 1964, the noted typographer Jan Tschichold (1902–1974), best known as a proponent of *die neue typographie* in the Weimar period and for his redesign of Penguin books at the end of the 1940s, was invited by the a group of German master printers to design a typeface that could be manufactured for three modes of metal type composition: foundry, Linotype, and Monotype. The result, completed in 1967 and issued in a foundry version by Stempel and a machine version that worked for both Monotype and Linotype, was Sabon, a synthesis of types by Claude Garamont and Guillaume Le Bé (1523/1524–1598). It became an immediate classic.

Although Sabon was a success in both incarnations, the machine version was severely compromised due to the Linotype's duplexing requirements and kerning limitations. This was especially noticeable in the italic which was considerably wider than the foundry version. Unfortunately, when Sabon was converted to the PostScript format, it was the Linotype version that was used. In 2002 Linotype sought to rectify this mistake by commissioning Jean François Porchez (b.1964) to design Sabon Next. Porchez based his redesign not only on the foundry version of Tschichold's 1967 tripartite typeface, but also on Tschichold's sources: Garamont's romans in the 1592 Egenolff-Berner type specimen and Le Bé's 5-line Pica Roman (c.1598). It is a revival of a revival.

Sabon Next, issued in both text and display versions, includes letters (e.g. roman and italic **f**) that ignore the Linotype kerning and duplexing restrictions as well as ones based on Tschichold's solutions to those problems (found in Stylistic Set 5–Tschichold). Porchez also designed ligatures, swash letters and ornaments that were never present in the original Sabon but which can be found in 16th-century French typography.

Detail of Triple Canon by Guillaume Le Bé from *Modéles des Caracteres de l'Imprimerie…* by Pierre-Simon Fournier le jeune (Paris, 1742).

Sabon Next Display | Claude Garamont (Parangon, 1557), Guillaume Le Bé (5-line Pica, c. 1598) and
Jan Tschichold (Stempel, 1967) – Jean François Porchez (Linotype, 2002)

ABCDEFGHIJKLMNOPQQRSTUV
WXYZ&&ABCDEFGHIJKLMNOPQQRST
uvwxyz&abcdeffghijklmnopqrsſtuvw
xyzaenru Thɗffffﬁﬁﬂﬂﬅﬃﬄﬃ ﬄﬆß
ﬅﬁ ﬆ ﬁM 1234567890 1234567890
{[(.,;:!?*)]}¶

COMPARISON: **G**, **a**, **f** from Triple Canon by Le Bé and **S**, **a**, **f** from a specimen of Stempel Sabon vs. Sabon Next Display (BELOW).

Haultin

Tros Anchiſiade, facilis deſcenſus Auerni :
Noctes, atque dies patet atri ianua Ditis :
Sed reuocare gradum , ſuperasq́. euadere ad auras
Hoc opus, hic labor eſt . paŭci, quos æquus amauit
Iupiter, aut ardens euexit ad æthera uirtus,
Dijs geniti potuere . tenent media omnia ſiluæ,
Cocytusq́. ſinu labens circumfluit atro.
Quòd ſi tantus amor menti, ſi tanta cupido eſt,
Bis Stygios innare lacus, bis nigra uidere
Tartara; & inſano iuuat indulgere labori :
Accipe, quæ peragenda prius . latet arbore opaca
Aureus & folijs, & lento uimine ramus,
Iunoni infernæ dictus ſacer . hunc tegit omnis

MvB Verdigris by Mark van Bronkhorst, like Adobe Garamond, has a roman and italic designed by different punchcutters but used together. Both are based on types used by Paulus Manutius (son of Aldus Manutius) for a 1584 edition of Caesar's *Commentaries on the Gallic War*: a roman by Granjon and a Pica Italic (c. 1557) by Pierre Haultin. Although not as celebrated as his contemporaries Claude Garamont and Robert Granjon, Haultin was equally talented. He is recognized as a master of small-sized typefaces.

It was precisely this aspect of Haultin's work that attracted van Bronkhorst. MvB Verdigris, although now supplemented by a display version, was origi-nally designed as an optically scaled text typeface, tai-lored for use at 9 pt. Its heaviness—in comparison to other revivals of 16th-century French typefaces such as Adobe Garamond—is deliberate. Van Bronkhorst has augmented Haultin's characters with a set of ligatures that includes some unusual but functional combina-tions (e.g., **TT**, **Th**, **Wh**, **gg**, **gy**, and **tt**), but otherwise has avoided excessive modernization. Note the palmate **Y**, question mark and curly brackets.

The same Haultin italic was revived by Matthew Carter when he was designing Galliard in the 1970s. Named Rochelle, it was never released.

Italic from *J. Caesaris Commentarii...* (Venice: Paulus Manutius, 1584).

MvB Verdigris Pro Text, Text Italic | Pierre Haultin (Pica Italic, 1557) – Mark van Bronkhorst (MvB Fonts, 2004)

ABCDEFGHIJKLMNOPQQRSTUV
WXYZ&ABCDEFGHIJKLMNOPQQRST
UVWXYZ&abcdefghijklmnopqrstuvwxyz
TT ThVhWh fb fff fh fi fj fk fl ft ffb ffh ffi ffj ffk ffl fft
gg ggy gy ß tt 1234567890 I1234567890
§[(.,;:!?)]?¶*

COMPARISON: **Q** , **u**, **fr** ligature by Haultin vs. MvB Verdigris Pro Text Italic. BELOW: Distinctive letters in MvB Verdigris Pro Text Italic.

Van Dijck

Auguftijn Romeyn.

ardius aliquanto moleftiufque cum OR AN
o acta res eft. Is enim reculia fcripferat, Ho
dis, Zelandifque atque Burgundis Præfe
n defignaret quando fe hifce prefecturis c
ffet Aperte InimicumNollet; cui Virium
k l m n o p q f s t v u w A B C D E F G H
C D E F G H I K L M N O P Q S T V U X Y Z

Auguftijn Curfijf.

Eadem, is admonenti Gubernatrici ut abire
ftelodamo, non modo non a paruerit, fed etia
fillum a Guberna trice Turrium a fecretis

Christoffel van Dijck was considered by Joseph Moxon, author of *Mechanick Exercises* (1683–1684), to be the best punchcutter in the Netherlands in his time. Some two dozen of his roman and italic types appear in the 1681 type specimen issued by the widow of Daniel Elsevier. Two of them, the Augustijn Romeyn and Cursijf, provided the starting point for Custodia by Fred Smeijers. Designed originally for the Custodia Foundation in Paris at the request of typographer Wigger Bierma, Custodia is a loose interpretation of these Van Dijck types. Smeijers and Bierma tossed in some personal preferences such as the inclusion of a small capital **Q** as the default lowercase **q**. Custodia is deliberately designed to be heavier than the digital version of Monotype Van Dijck (1937) and DTL Elzevir (1993), the only other modern revivals of Van Dijck's typefaces. The latter, designed by Gerard Daniëls (b. 1966), is a loose interpretation based on a collection of Van Dijck's types used by the Elseviers.

Although Van Dijck worked in the 17th century, his typefaces are closer in color and spirit to 16th-century French types such as those by Garamont than to those of his contemporaries, which tend to be darker, narrower, and have a taller x-height (a combination often described by type historians as *le goût Hollandois*).

Detail from the broadside *Proeven van Letteren* issued by the widow of Daniel Elsevier (1681) showing the typefaces of Christoffel Van Dijck.

Custodia Pro | Christoffel van Dijck (1650s) – Fred Smeijers (Our Type, 2002)

ABCDEFGHIJKLMNOPQRSTUVWX
YZ&ABCDEFGHIJKLMNOPQRSTUVWXYZ&
abcdefghijklmnopqqrsſtuvwxyzfffiflffiffl
1234567890**1234567890**{[(.,;:!?★)]}¶

DTL Elzevir and DTL Elzevir Alternates | Christoffel van Dijck (17th c.) – Gerard Daniëls (Dutch Type Library, 1993)

ABCDEFGHIJKLMNOPQRSTUVW
XYZ&abcdefghijklmnopqrstuvvwxyz
a e i m n t u Thctfffiflfrftfſtstffiffl
1234567890**1234567890**{[(.,;:!?★)]}¶

COMPARISON: **A, G, a, g** from Augustijn Romeyn by Van Dijck vs. Custodia Pro.

Jannon

La crainte de l'Eternel eſt le chef de ſcience : mais les fols meſpriſent ſapièce & inſtruction. Mon fils, eſcoute l'inſtruction de ton pere, & ne delaiſſe point l'enſeignemẽt de ta mere.

Car ils ſeront graces enfilees enſemble à ton chef, & carquans à ton col. Mon fils, ſi les

Jannon Antiqua Pro | Jean Jannon (1621) – František Štorm (Storm Typefoundry, 2010)

ABCDEFGHIJKLMNOPQRSTU
VWXYZ&ABCDEFGHIJKLMNOPQRSTUV
wxyz&abcdefghijklmnopqrsſtuvwxyz
ThTiWhchckctfbffffhfifjfkflftffbffhffiffj
ffkfflfftofoffoffiſpſtſhſiſlſttt
1234567890{[(.,;:!?*)]}¶

Jean Jannon was a Protestant printer in Sedan, France. His 1621 type specimen is the source of Jannon Antiqua Pro by František Štorm (b. 1966). It hews closely to Jannon's design, though the character set has been enhanced by the addition of a wide array of ligatures, some of them modern (e.g., **Th**) and some of them quirky (e.g., **offi**).

Matrices for Jannon's roman and italic types (Gros Canon, Petit Canon and Gros Parangon) were purchased by the Imprimerie Royale in 1641 where they became known as the *Caractères de l'Université*. In a series of books published between 1900 and 1904, Arthur Christian (1838–1906), director of the Imprimerie Nationale (successor to the Imprimerie Royale) mistook them for types by Garamont, unwittingly sparking a string of "false" Garamonds issued by a horde of type manufacturers over the course of the 20th century.

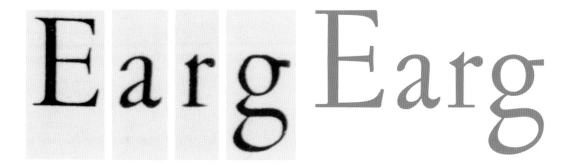

OPPOSITE: Detail from *The 1621 Specimen of Jean Jannon, Paris and Sedan, Designer and Engraver of the "Caractères de L'Université"*... Beatrice Warde (Paris: H. Champion, 1927).
COMPARISON (ABOVE): **E, a, r, g** from Jannon specimen vs. Jannon Pro.

Benton

COMBINING the qualities of force and elegance in an exceptional degree, this beautiful letter designed by the first professional type founder in the year 1540 presents opportunities for the widest range of application to the intelligent printer of to-day Its utility and beauty will make it a standard type of the future.

Detail from the first complete display of the Garamond Series in the *Specimen Book and Catalogue 1923* (Jersey City, New Jersey: American Type Founders Company, 1923), p. 20.

COMPARISON (OPPOSITE): **a**, **r**, **g** from ATF Garamond specimen vs. ATF Garamond Subhead. BELOW: Distinctive characters in MvB Verdigris Italic.

ATF Garamond Subhead | Jean Jannon (1621) and Morris Fuller Benton (American Type Founders, 1919) –
Mark van Bronkhorst (ATF, 2015)

ABCDEFGHIJKLMNOPQRSTUV
WXYZ&ABCDEFGHIJKLMNOPQRST
UVWXYZ&abcdefghijklmnopqrstuvw
xyzaㄷᴇᴍᴨᴜᴜᴄ̃tfbff fh fifjfkflftffbffh
ffiffjffkfflfft ſt tt {[[(.,;:!?*)]]}ᵷ
11234567890O1234567890

The first of the revived "Garamonds" based on Jannon was ATF Garamond by Morris Fuller Benton (1872–1948), with swash capitals and decorative elements by T.M. Cleland (1880–1964), released in 1919. It was heavier in weight and softer in appearance than Jannon's original design. It quickly became a success and was soon followed by other "Garamonds" based on Jannon from Monotype Corporation, Lanston Monotype,

Ludlow, Mergenthaler Linotype, and various other foundries. Benton's design has been revived by Mark van Bronkhorst, now the owner of the American Type Founders name and rights, in a series of optical sizes (excluding display). ATF Garamond includes the full Benton and Cleland character set, thus making it the best of the "false" Garamonds available today.

ste

ABCD
EGHK
abcdeg

ABCDE
FGHIJK
abcdefgh

Dutch Oldstyle Types

¶ Robert Granjonworked for Christophe Plantin, the Antwerp printer, for nine years beginning in 1563. He was succeeded as Plantin's chief supplier of types by Hendrik van den Keere, who cut romans, italics, texturas, and music type. Several of van den Keere's romans (e.g., 2-line Canon and Ascendonica), presumably influenced by Granjon's, are considered to be the earliest examples of what has since come to be known as *le goût hollandois* or Dutch Oldstyle. They share the same dark color, tall x-height, and sharp serifs.

Van den Keere was at the forefront of a shift in the influence of type design from France to the Low Countries that lasted into the early 18th century. It was occasioned by the rise of Holland as a leading mercantile nation. In the 17th century, the reputation of Dutch printing was spread throughout Europe by the Elsevier dynasty of printers, whose compact books, printed in a range of languages, were designed in a consistent format and overwhelmingly printed—contrary to common belief—in French (or French-influenced) types rather than Dutch ones. But from the 1660s on, the books of less celebrated Dutch printers began to employ local types that are darker in appearance due to a larger x-height and narrower body.

Purveyors of this new Dutch style were the Voskens family of punchcutters of whom Dirk Voskens (1647–1691) is the best known. He is credited with teaching punchcutting to Miklós Kis (1650–1702), a Transylvanian who had traveled to Amsterdam in 1680 to learn the art of printing. Kis' types, rediscovered in the 20th century under the name of Janson, have been considered by some to be the best types ever cut.

As Dutch types came to the fore, English printers began to import them (or sets of Dutch matrices). This was spurred by State censorship which restricted printing to London, Cambridge, and Oxford. Furthermore, the Star Chamber decree of 1637, which was in effect for most of the remainder of the century, limited the number of typefounders in England to four. In 1676 Dr. John Fell (1625–1686), Dean of Christ Church and later Bishop of Oxford, hired Peter de Walpergen (1646–1703), a German-born Dutch punchcutter, to cast type. After 1690, Walpergen was also paid to cut type, including large sizes of roman and italic. Although Walpergen

OPPOSITE: Five Lines Pica and Four Lines Pica from *A Specimen of Printing Types, by W. Caslon and Son, Letter Founders, in London* (London: Printed by Dryden Leach, 1764).

has been described as a punchcutter of the second rank, he was apparently better than any of the native English cutters, including Joseph Moxon (1627–1691), author of the important treatise *Mechanick Exercises: Or, the Doctrine of Handy-Works Applied to the Art of Printing* (1683). In 1693 Bishop Fell acquired some excellent small types cut by Christoffel Van Dijck and Dirk Voskens for use at the Oxford Press. Along with the types cut by Walpergen these came to be known as the Fell types.

The Glorious Revolution of 1688 removed restrictions on the printing trade. But there were not enough trained punch-cutters in England to meet the demand for new types of quality. At the beginning of the 18th century Dutch types continued to dominate English printing. Around 1720, the London printer William Bowyer (1663–1737), having become upset by this situation, led an effort to finance the training of William Caslon (1692–1766), an engraver of ornamental gunlocks, as a punchcutter. Caslon's first roman and italic, cut in 1722, were immediately received as superior to anything then available in England.

Over the next decade Caslon developed the best-stocked foundry in England. He issued a broadside specimen sheet in 1734 showing fourteen sizes of roman and italic types, all influenced by Dutch types. For instance, his Great Primer roman was modeled at a distance, in the words of historian James Mosley (b. 1935), on the Text Romeyn of Nicolas Briot (c. 1585–1626), the chief supplier of types in the 1620s to the Amsterdam printer Willem Janszoon Blaeu (1571–1638). However, historian Daniel Berkeley Updike (1860–1941) and others believe that Caslon's types surpassed those of his Dutch progenitors. For most of the remainder of the 18th century, Caslon's types dominated printing in England and in the American colonies. Their success stopped the importation of Dutch types, but continued the influence of the Dutch style.

Although Caslon's types had fallen out of favor by the 1790s, they were revived in the 1840s by the publisher William Pickering (1796–1854) and his printer Charles Whittingham (1795–1876) who first used them in *The Diary of Lady Willoughby* (1844). Sometime between 1878 and 1884, H. W. Caslon & Co., responding to the slowly growing interest in the original Caslon types, renamed them Caslon Oldface. But the types they issued, as typographer and historian Justin Howes (1963–2005) and James Mosley have pointed out, were "modernized" with the punches recut and the type machine-cast to make the letters crisper and smoother. These are the Caslon types that came to be popular in the United States in the first half of the 20th century.

This chapter emphasizes revivals of the romans of van den Keere, Kis and Caslon.

THE ORIGINAL
CASLON
OLDSTYLE

THIS is the only ORIGINAL Caslon. First cast in this country, by MacKellar, Smiths & Jordan over *forty years ago;* original matrices from punches cut by William Caslon, in 1722. *This* Caslon Series has never been duplicated—nor imitated.... Every large publishing house remembers this fact, and uses these exquisitely cut letters by Caslon

AMERICAN TYPE
FOUNDERS COMPANY

An advertisement for the Original Caslon Old Style from American Type Founders in *The Inland Printer* (1901).

Van den Keere

A B C D E F
G H I K L M N
O P Q R S T
V X Y Z

a b c d e f g h i j k l
m n o p q r ſ s t u v
x , y ; z . ę : 1 ?

Renard no. 1 | Hendrik van den Keere (2-line Canon Roman, 1570) – Fred Smeijers (TEFF, 1998)

ABCDEFGHIJKLMNOPQQRSTU VWXYZ&ABCDEFGHIJKLMNOPQQR STUVWXYZ&abcdefghijklmnopqrstu vwxyzffffffffflfffffff 12345678900{[(.,;:!?*)]}¶

Hendrik van den Keere was the best punchcutter of the Low Countries in the 16th century. He began working for the Antwerp printer Christophe Plantin in 1568, and after 1570 was his sole supplier of types. His larger romans, characterized by a tall x-height, narrow proportion and dark color, marked a break with the French Oldstyle romans of Garamont et al. His 2-line Canon Roman (1570) was one of the largest romans cut in the 16th century to have a lowercase.

Fred Smeijers discovered van den Keere's 2-line Canon Roman while doing research at the Plantin-Moretus Museum in 1987/1988. His revival of it, called Renard, was used to set his book *Counterpunch: Making Type in the Sixteenth Century, Designing Typefaces Now* (1996) before being released commercially by The Enschedé Font Foundry. The lowercase is a close revival while the capitals are more interpretive and the italic is entirely Smeijers' own invention. Renard comes in three numbered weight variations with the darkest (no. 1) being closest to van den Keere's roman.

Quarto, designed by Sara Soskolne (b. 1970) at Hoefler & Co., borrows from three of van den Keere's types (the 7-line Canon Roman, 2-line Great Primer Roman and 2-line Canon Roman). It is sharper and has stronger stroke contrast than Renard. The medium weight is the closest to van den Keere's 2-line Canon Roman. The rest of the family was extrapolated from this weight while the italic was invented entirely by Soskolne. Both Renard and Quarto are notable for their restrained character set.

DTL VandenKeere by Frank Blokland (b. 1959) is based on van den Keere's Parangonne Roman (c. 1575), a smaller and lighter face than his 2-line Pica Roman. It is closer in color and style to contemporary French romans. Blokland believes Garamont's Parangon Roman (see pp. 51–52) served as its template. For the italic of DTL VandenKeere Blokland chose François Guyot's Ascendonica Cursive (c. 1557) as a model. Thus, DTL VandenKeere can more properly be classified as a French Oldstyle.

OPPOSITE: Detail of 2-line Canon Roman by Hendrik van den Keere (1570) from punches at the Plantin-Moretus Museum.

G G G

g g g

a a a

Quarto Medium | Hendrik van den Keere (2-line Canon Roman, 1570) – Sara Soskolne (Hoefler & Co., 2014)

ABCDEFGHIJJKLMNOPQRSTUV
WXYZ&abcdefghijklmnopqrstuvwxyz
fb ff fh fi fj fk fl ffb ffh ffi ffj ffk ffl
1234567890123456890{[(.,;:!?*)]}¶

DTL VandenKeere D | Hendrik van den Keere (Parangonne Roman, c. 1575) – (Dutch Type Library, 1995)

ABCDEFGHIJKLMNOPQRSTUV
WXYZ&ABCDEFGHIJKLMNOPQRSTU
vwxyzabcdefghijklmnopqrstuvwxyz
fi fl 1234567890123456890{[(.,;:!?*)]}¶

COMPARISON: **h** from 2-line Canon Roman by van den Keere vs. Renard No. 1 | Renard No. 2 | Renard No. 3.

Kis

Miklós Kis, was sent by the leaders of the Reformed Church in Transylvania to Amsterdam in 1680 to print the Bible in Hungarian. While there he learned punch-cutting and typefounding, probably from Dirk Voskens. His types, displayed in a broadside specimen, are more consistent in design from size to size than those of previous punchcutters. (Shown here is his Kleine Canon roman taken from a book printed by Kis in 1696.) His italics are among the first to have a greater regularity of slope. Kis sold matrices of his types to the Erhardt foundry in Leipzig. When they were rediscovered in the 20th century by Stempel, which had acquired the Erhardt material, they were misattributed to the Leipzig typefounder Anton Janson (1620–1687). Proper credit to

Kis only came in the 1950s through the efforts of typographer György Haiman (1914–1996).

Kis Antiqua Now was designed originally in 1988 by Hildegard Korger (b.1935), a calligrapher and lettering artist, for VEB Typoart, the East German foundry. Two decades later, she redesigned it, in collaboration with Erhard Kaiser (b.1957), as a digital type. It is considered to be the best digital interpretation of Kis' types available today, successfully capturing their sturdy elegance, while also meeting the needs of contemporary reading habits and fields of application. It has a large glyph palette that includes long **s** ligatures and quaint ligatures; and, in the italic, a full set of swash capitals. There are headline and body copy versions.

Detail of Kleine Canon roman typeface by Miklos Kis. From a 1696 imprint.

Kis Antiqua Now TH Pro | Miklós Kis (1690s) – Hildegard Korger with Erhard Kaiser (Elsner + Flake, 2008)

ABCDEFGHIJKLMNOPQRSTUV
WXYZ&ABCDEFGHIJKLMNOPQRSTUV
wxyz&abcdefghijklmnopqrſstuvwxyz
ſtff fi fj fl ft ffi ffj ff st ſt tt ſſ ſi ſj ſl ſt ſſi tt
11234567890 1234567890{[(.,;:!?*)]}

agk agk

agk agk

COMPARISON: **a**, **g**, **k** from Kleine Canon roman by Kis vs. Kis Antiqua Now; BELOW: Erhardt vs. Janson Text 55.

Caslon

Two Lines Great Primer.

ousque tanc

itere Catilin

ousque tander

ere, Catilina,

Two Lines Englifh.

ousque tandem

, Catilina, pati

ra? quamdiu n

usque tandem ab

lina, patientia no

Two Lines Pica.

usque tandem ab

ina, patientia noftra

William Caslon was originally trained as a metal worker with expertise in engraving gunlocks. His foundry, set up in 1720, was financed by several London printers eager to have a domestic source of quality type as an alternative to Dutch imports. His types followed the prevailing Dutch style. However, unlike those of Kis, they vary considerably in design from size to size.

The four sizes of ITC Founder's Caslon are a small part of an extensive attempt by Justin Howes to faithfully capture Caslon's variations. Howes, having purchased the rights to the remnants of H. W. Caslon & Co., printed letterpress samples of each size of type; then digitized the results, leaving the characters as they were, warts and all. However, the types in the ITC Founder's Caslon family are not necessarily identical to those cut by Caslon himself since, as James Mosley has pointed out, Caslon punches were recut and sharpened in the second half of the 19th century to accommodate printers used to the brilliance of neoclassical types.

Carol Twombly, the designer of Adobe Caslon, took a different approach than Howes. Rather than try to recreate a specific size of Caslon's oeuvre, she chose to achieve the Caslon "look" through a synthesis of several of his smaller types (English Roman no. 2, Pica Roman nos. 1 and 2, Small Pica Roman no. 2, Long Primer Roman no. 1, and Brevier Roman no. 2). Similarly, Matthew Carter based his Big Caslon on several of Caslon's largest sizes of type: most notably Five Lines Pica and Four Lines Pica. Consequently, Adobe Caslon is most successful when used for text, while Big Caslon is at its best in display situations.

There are other notable digital interpretations of Caslon's types, each designed from a different perspective. See King's Caslon (Dalton Maag, 2007) by Marc Weymann and Ron Carpenter; Williams Caslon (Font Bureau, 2010) by William Berkson; and William by Maria Doreuli (Typotheque, 2016).

ITC Founder's Caslon Twelve | William Caslon (1734) – Justin Howes (ITC, 1998)

ABCDEFGHIJKLMNOPQRSTUV
WXYZ&ABCDEFGHIJKLMNOPQRSTUVWX
yz&abcdefghijklmnopqrstuvwxyz
&ct ff fi fl ffi ffl fh fi ft 1234567890 {[(.,;:!?*)]}

ITC Founder's Caslon Thirty | William Caslon (1734) – Justin Howes (ITC, 1998)

ABCDEFGHIJKLMNOPQRSTUV
WXYZ&ABCDEFGHIJKLMNOPQRSTUVW
XYZ&abcdefghijklmnopqrstuvwxyz
&ct ff fi fl ffi ffl fh fi ft 1234567890{[(.,;:!?*)]}

ITC Founder's Caslon Poster & Ornaments | William Caslon (1734) – Justin Howes (ITC, 1998)

ABCDEFGHIJKLMNOPQRSTUVW
XYZ&abcdefghijklmnopqrstuvwxyz
&ct ff fi fl ffi ffl fh fi ft 1234567890 {[(.,;:!?*)]}

OPPOSITE: Detail of Two Lines Great Primer, Two Lines English, and Two Lines Pica from *A Specimen of Printing Types, by W. Caslon and Son, Letter Founders, in London* (London: Printed by Dryden Leach, 1764). .

CCCC

kkkk

a a a a

a a

Adobe Caslon Pro | William Caslon (1730s–1760s) – Carol Twombly (Adobe, 1991)

ABCDEFGHIJKLMNOPQRSTUV
WXYZ&ABCDEFGHIJKLMNOPQRSTUV
wxyz&abcdefghijklmnopqrsſtuvwxyz
Thﬀﬁﬃﬄﬅﬂﬃﬃﬃﬄststﬆﬃﬀﬃﬃ
1234567890I234567890{[(.,;:!?*)]}¶

Big Caslon | William Caslon – Matthew Carter (Carter & Cone, 1994)

ABCDEFGHIJJKLMNOPQQR
STUVWXYZ&&ABCDEFGHIJKLMN
OPQRSTUVWXYZ&abcdefghijklmnopq
rsſtuvwxyzﬅﬀﬁﬃﬄﬃﬄﬃﬄﬃﬄﬃﬄﬃﬄﬃ
stﬃﬄﬅ1234567890{[(.,;:!?*)]}¶

ABOVE: Four types by Caslon (FROM LEFT TO RIGHT): English Roman no. 2, Pica Roman no. 1, Pica Roman no. 2, and Small Pica Roman no. 2 from *A Specimen of Printing Types, by W. Caslon and Son, Letter Founders, in London* (London: Printed by Dryden Leach, 1764).

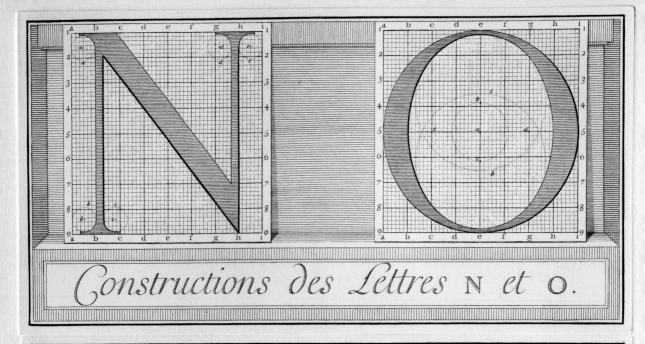

Constructions des Lettres N et O.

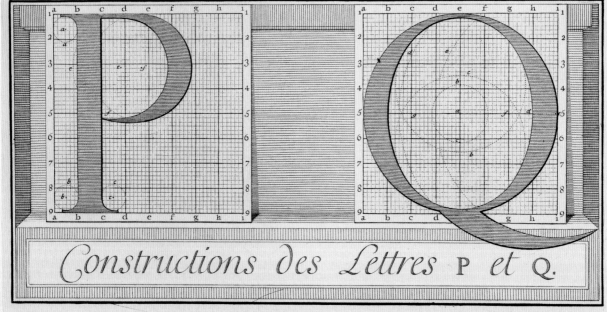

Constructions des Lettres P et Q.

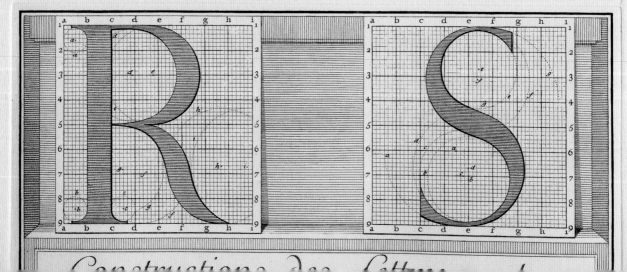

Constructions des Lettres

Transitional Types

Transitional types are not a cohesive group of types with common features, but a set of designs that represent different points on a style spectrum with oldstyle types at one end and modern ones at the other. Each transitional type is in flux in its own way, with differing degrees of change in stroke contrast, stress, serif structure and, in the italic, cursiveness. Viewed in this manner, the larger Caslon types could arguably be classed as transitional (see p. 70).

The transitional period begins in the 1690s with the design and cutting of the Romain du Roi, a new typeface for the exclusive use of the Imprimerie Royale and ends in the 1780s with the emergence of the modern types of Firmin Didot (1764–1836) in France and Giambattista Bodoni (1740–1813) in Italy. The Romain du Roi was designed along rational lines, with the broad-edged pen of the calligrapher and the graver of the punchcutter being replaced by mathematical formulas—though the actual types cut by Philippe Grandjean (1666–1714) relied heavily on the eye and hand. The type was marked by strong stroke contrast, minimally bracketed serifs (double-sided for the lowercase ascenders), **b, d, p** and **q** as a single design mirrored and rotated, and a sloped roman for the italic. In France, the Romain du Roi influenced Pierre-Simon Fournier le jeune (1712–1768) whose romans, first shown in a 1742 specimen, broke from the still-prevalent Garamont types to follow the shift toward greater stroke contrast and thinner, sharper serifs.

In Holland, the transitional style was represented by the types of Johann Michel Fleischmann (1701–1768), which in the 1730s and 1740s veered away from the Dutch style of Voskens et al with increased stroke contrast, reduced bracketing of serifs on capitals, the addition of exaggerated spurs on several letters, and the replacement of lobes with ball terminals. In England, the amateur printer John Baskerville (1706–1775) designed types inspired by his early experience as a writing master. His roman letters, influenced by the pressure and release technique of the pointed, flexible nib, are characterized by lightness, quickness of weight transition, fullness of curve, vertical bias, and tighter bracketing of serifs.

These types were influenced by different environments and factors, but they all tended to move, at varying degrees of speed, toward the neoclassical types of Didot and Bodoni.

OPPOSITE: Detail of construction of the letters **N**, **O**, **P**, **Q, R** and **S**. Plate engraved by Louis Simonneau (1695). From *La réforme de la typographie royale sous Louis XIV. Le Grandjean* by André Jammes (Paris: Librairie Paul Jammes, 1961).

Grandjean

un Royaume, leRoy eſtablit, ſous
e Aſſemblée particuliére de ce qu'
n Géométrie, en Aſtronomie, en
rmie; pour perfectionner ces Scien
itions au public. Ils s'aſſembloient
1. Enſuite Sa Majeſté leur a donné
vre, où deux fois la ſemaine ils tie
a produit un grand nombre de re

In 1692, a commission appointed by the Académie Royale des Sciences and directed by Abbé Jean-Paul Bignon (1662–1743) to make the Description des Arts et Métiers decided to make a new set of types for the project. Philippe Grandjean, who held the title of *graveur du roi*, was given the task. The first punches were apparently cut in 1696, following a design created by the commission. The design was unusual in that it was done mathematically. The roman capitals, engraved as large copperplate prints by Louis Simonneau (1654–1727) as early as 1695, were constructed on a square divided into a grid of sixty-four units, each of which was further subdivided into thirty-six smaller units for a total of 2,304 tiny squares. A coarser grid was designed for the lowercase. The italic letterforms were constructed on a rhombus divided in a similar manner. However, the actual types cut by Grandjean are less rigid.

The first appearance of sizes of the Romain du roi, as it came to be known, was in *Médailles sur le Principaux Evénements du Règne de Louis le Grand…* (1702). Ultimately, the Romain du Roi comprised 21 different bodies of roman and italic, and 20 bodies of roman and italic intials. Grandjean cut a total of fourteen sizes of the Romain du Roi before his death, with the remaining sizes being cut first by his pupil and assistant Jean Alexandre and then by Alexandre's son-in-law, Louis Luce (d. 1773). The entire project was completed in 1745.

Romain by Ian Party, available in headline and text versions, is not a close copy of the Romain du roi. It lacks the distinctive spur on the lowercase l, and the unusual double head serifs on the lowercase ascenders have been replaced with conventional ones. These changes make Romain a more functional typeface than if it was historically accurate.

Detail of the Romain du Roi from *Médailles sur les Principaux Evenements du Regne de Louis le Grand…* (Paris: Imprimerie Royale, 1702).

Romain Regular | Philippe Grandjean (1702) – Ian Party (BP Type Foundry, 2007)

ABCDEFGHIJKLMNOPQRS
TUVWXYZ&abcdefghijklmno
pqrstuvwxyzff fi fl ffi ffl
1234567890123456 7890{[(.,;:!?*)]}

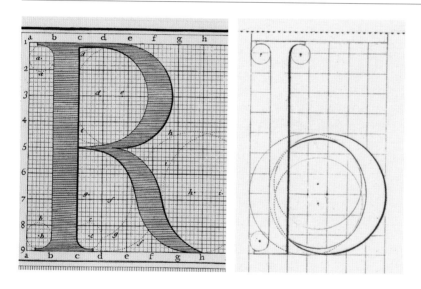

ABOVE: **R** , **b** engraved by Louis Simonneau with two different grids.
COMPARISON (BELOW): **R, b, l** from Romain du Roi typeface vs. BP Romain Regular.

Fournier

villes, & de plusieurs autres
mée lui ayant déferé le titre
mort de Neron , il refusa lo
dignité ; mais l'ayant enfin
Commandement des Trou
chever l'expedition de Jud

Pierre-Simon Fournier le jeune set up his own foundry in 1736, independent of the one run by his brother Jean-Pierre Fournier l'aîné. His roman types followed the new style established by the Romain du Roi while his italics reflected the influence of contemporary French scripts. The romans are distinguished by minimally bracketed serifs, except for the slightly beaked head serifs of the stems of lowercase letters, a relatively tall x-height, and variable stress on curved letters (e.g., **c** is canted while **o** is vertical). In the continuum of transitional typefaces, Fournier falls on the end closest to the moderns.

The first revival of Fournier's types was made by the Monotype Corporation in 1925 as part of Stanley Morison's (1889–1967) celebrated "Programme of Typographical Design". But the design issued was a mistake. Uncertain of the details he wanted in the typeface, Morison had ordered the Type Drawing Office to prepare two versions of Fournier's types, one named Barbou (after the printer of Fournier's type specimens) and the other Fournier (based on the St. Augustin or 14 pt type). Although Morison preferred Barbou, it was the Fournier that somehow was put into production, where it has remained ever since despite changes in type technology.

In its Text and Petit optical styles PS Fournier by Stéphane Elbaz (b. 1975) is the first revival of Fournier to capture the proper flavor of the original. The sharpness and high contrast of Grand, the third optical size, gives PS Fournier a more neoclassical appearance. The glyph palette of each version contains several alternates (e.g., two forms of **b**) as well as a large set of ligatures that includes archaic and modern forms.

Detail of Cicero Ordinaire by Pierre-Simon Fournier le jeune from *Modéles des Caractéres de l'Imprimerie... by Pierre-Simon Fournier le jeune* (Paris, 1742).

PS Fournier Pro Regular | Pierre-Simon Fournier le jeune (1740s) – Stephane Elbaz (Typofonderie, 2016)

AABCDEFGHIJKLMNOPQQRST
UVWWXYZ&ABCDEFGHIJKLMNOPQ
QRSTUVWXYZ&abbcdefghijklmnopq
qrstuvwxyzTh&ct fb ff fh fi fj fk fl ft ffb ffh
ffi ffj ffk ffl fft st fb fh fi fj fk fl fft ffb ffh ffi
ffj ffk ffl fft {[(.,;:!?*)]}¶
1234567890 1234567890

COMPARISON (ABOVE): **G, a** from Cicero Ordinaire by Fournier vs. PS Fournier Pro Regular.
COMPARISON (BELOW): PS Fournier Pro Grand | PS Fournier Pro Regular | PS Fournier Pro Petit.

Fleischmann

lui donner moins de vingt ans à l[a]
mort de Cyrus :　elle avoit don[c]
foixante - quinze ans lors qu'u[n]
nouveau Roi la demande comm[e]
une grace particuliere.　PLTGA[

ABCDEFHIJKMNOQSU
VWXYZÆ ÆABCDEFGHIJK[
MMNOPQRSTUVWYZ ÇĒŌ[v]
1234567891ot([ſ]§!?aóſúmi

J. M. Fleifchman fculpfit. 1739.

Johann Michael Fleischmann was a German-born punchcutter who spent most of his career in Amsterdam, where he cut punches for several foundries, most importantly that of Johannes Enschedé (1708–1780). Beginning with their 1768 specimen book, the Enschedé foundry promoted him assiduously. Fleischmann's types are at the oldstyle end of the transitional continuum. In the German type classification scheme they are considered baroque, a term that aptly describes many of their features such as the spiky spur serifs on many of the capitals, the unusual tail of **Q**, and the ball terminals on several lowercase letters.

Fleischmann's types were copied closely by Jacques-François Rosart (1714–1777) of Brussels, but had little influence outside of the Low Countries. Prior to the design of DTL Fleischmann by Erhard Kaiser, the only modern revival of Fleischmann was Fleischmann-Antiqua created by Georg Belwe (1878–1954) for the Ludwig Wagner foundry in 1928. DTL Fleischmann has display and text sizes, both apparently based on Fleischmann's Augustijn Romeyn, which Enschedé says was cut in 1738. Although the form of the letters is very accurate, the stroke contrast, even in the display version, seems less sprightly than Fleischmann's original.

More recently, both Mercury (1997) by Jonathan Hoefler (b. 1970) and Tobias Frere-Jones (b. 1970), and Freight (2004–2009) by Joshua Darden (b. 1979) have been heavily influenced by Fleischmann.

Detail of Text Romeyn cut in 1739 by Johann Michael Fleischmann from *Proef van Letteren… Lettergietery van J. Enschedé* (Haarlem, 1768).

DTL Fleischmann D | Johann Michael Fleischmann (1730s) – Erhard Kaiser (Dutch Type Library, 1992)

ABCDEFGHIJKLMNOPQRST
UVWXYZ&ABCDEFGHIJKLMNOP
QRSTUVWXYZ&abcdefghijklmnopq
rsſtuvwxyzctffſtffiffffſtſſſiſlſtſſiſl
ſhſkſlſpſtthtt{[(.,;:!?*)]}¶
1234567890 1234567890

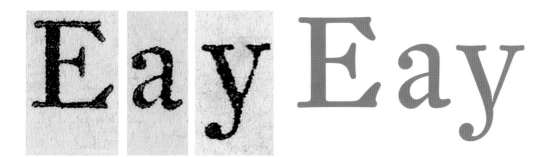

QRg

COMPARISON: **E**, **a**, **y** from Text Romeyn by Fleischmann vs. DTL Fleischmann D. BELOW: Distinctive letters from DTL Fleischmann D.

Pradell

con su gente á gana

quando los Egipciano

n su tierra tan pobr

ido, y mal ataviad

bantáron mucho; y e

el Rey de Egipto, ll

o, como le vido ta

le cuerpo, y tan m

Eudald Pradell (1721–1788) became a punchcutter at the urging of Pablo Barra, the head of the Imprenta Real in Barcelona. His first type was the Peticano, cut in 1758. He cut three others (Lectura, Texto, and Entredos) while in Barcelona. In 1764 King Carlos III gave him a pension on the condition that he move his foundry to Madrid.

Pradell's types, shown in a specimen issued by his widow in 1793, are characterized by a large x-height, and details taken from the types of Fournier (e.g., the serifs of the lowercase) and Fleischmann (e.g., the serifs on **E**, **F**, **L** and **T**). Mário Feliciano (b. 1969) designed Eudald, based on Pradell's work, in 1998. He revised the design in 2006 for newspaper use and renamed it Eudald News. It first appeared in the Portuguese daily newspaper *Diário de Notícías*. Eudald News is part of the foundry's Iberian Historical Series, which, along with Rongel (2001), Merlo (2004), and Geronimo (2010), celebrates the golden era of Spanish typography in the 18th century.

Detail of Atanasia Chica (plate no. VIII) from *Muestras de los Grados de Letras . . . de Fundicion de la Viuda é Hijo de Pradell* (Madrid: En la Oficina de Don Benito Cano, 1793).

Eudald News | Eudald Pradell (1750s) – Mário Feliciano (Feliciano Typefoundry, 1998)

ABCDEFGHIJKLMNOPQRSTUV
WXYZ&&ABCDEFGHIJKLMNOPQRS
TUVWXYZ&abcdefghijklmnopqrstuv
wxyzff fi fj fl ffi ffl {[(.,;:!?*)]}¶¶
123456789012 34567890

COMPARISON: **E, g, c, a** from Atanasia Chica by Pradell vs. Eudald News. BELOW: Distinctive letters from Eudald News.

Baskerville

Illi inter ſeſe duri cer
Contulerant: media
Namque ut ab Evand
Regem adit, et Regi
Quidve petat, quidve

John Baskerville, having made his fortune in the japan-ning trade, retired from business and around 1750 turned his attention to printing. He set up a paper mill, printing office and type foundry in his hometown of Birmingham, England, and began to print books, the first being a Virgil in 1757. He designed a new style of type, influenced by his early career as a writing master, which was lighter and more open than the prevailing Caslon types. The fruit of nearly eight years of exper-imentation, its qualities were enhanced by the rich black ink and innovative hot-pressed rag paper he used in his printing. Baskerville's types were cut by John Handy (d. 1792).

Baskerville 10 Pro by František Štorm, based on Baskerville's Great Primer Roman, is the most accu-rate digital version available today. However, the char-acter set has a number of modern ligatures, some of them peculiar.

Mrs. Eaves, the first foray by Zuzana Licko (b. 1961) into historically influenced types, is an homage to Baskerville more than a revival. The letters have a lower stroke contrast, smaller x-height, and chunkier serifs. Licko has said that her goal was to make Baskerville more readable. Mrs. Eaves is supplemented by "petit caps" and a large set of "smart" ligatures (designed in conjunction with Just van Rossum [b. 1966] and Erik van Blokland [b. 1967] of Letterror). The latter includes a number of functionally useless forms such as **ee**, **gi** and **ip**. The typeface is named after Baskerville's housekeeper- turned-wife.

Detail from p. 347 of *Bucolica, Georgica et Aeneis* by Virgil (Birmingham: John Baskerville, 1757).

Baskerville 10 Pro | John Baskerville (1757) – František Štorm (Storm Typefoundry, 2010)

ABCDEFGHIJKLMNOPQRSTU
VWXYZ&ABCDEFGHIJKLMNOPQRS
TUVWXYZ&abcdefghijklmnopqrstu
vwxyzThTiTTTTYWhctffffifjfkflftof
ſpſtſhſiſlſtffiffjffkfflfftoffofioffi
1234567890123456789o{[(.,;:!?*)]}

COMPARISON: **C**, **E**, **a**, **g** from Great Primer roman by Baskerville vs. Baskerville 10 Pro.

b b b

g g g

Q Q Q

Q

Mrs. Eaves | John Baskerville (1757) – Zuzana Licko (Emigre, 1996)

ABCDEFGHIJKLMNOPQRSTUVWX
YZ & ABCDEFGHIJKLMNOPQRSTUVWXYZ
ABCDEFGHIJKLMNOPQRSTUVWXYZabcdefghijk
lmnopqrstuvwxyzAAÆAVFFFFIFLHELA
VBBMDVEMPNKNTŒŒGGERTTTWTY
UBUDULUPURVATEThaecteefbfffhfiflftfy
gggigyipitkyœpyspstfsʃstttwtyckyffbffiffh
ffjfflffrfftffyggytty
1234567890I234567890{[(.,;:!?*)]}¶

Varieties of Mrs. Eaves Smart Ligatures: historical | practical | unnecessary | silly.

Moore · Austin

Eight Lines Pica.

ALTON
Coaches.

"[A]lthough his fonts never had much vogue in England," Daniel Berkeley Updike says of Baskerville, "they did have an enormous influence on the later development of English type-forms, and on the type-forms of Europe." Among the former are the types of Isaac Moore and Richard Austin (1756–1832).

Moore was the managing partner and punchcutter in a Bristol foundry begun in 1764 with the printer William Pine and Joseph Fry. The partnership was dissolved in 1776 but Moore's types continued to be sold by Edmund Fry (1754–1835) who took over the foundry from his father in 1787. Although openly described by Fry as copies of Baskerville's types, the Five Lines Pica and Four Lines Pica sizes are an original design. It was revived in the 20th century by Stephenson, Blake & Co. under the name of Fry's Baskerville. With Big Moore, Matthew Carter has restored Moore's authorship of these gorgeous letterforms. The character set includes alternate forms of **Q** and **&**; and unusual ligatures for **et** and **rt**.

Richard Austin (1756–1832) was a typefounder, punchcutter, wood engraver and painter. He cut the types of the British Letter-Foundry established by John Bell (d. 1831) in 1787. His types for Bell improved on the Baskerville model in sharpness of cutting and modeling of form. Within a decade the Bell type was eclipsed by neoclassical types, but it never fell entirely out of favor. It continued in use under various names in the United States and England in the 19th century, and in the 20th century it was rediscovered by both Updike and Bruce Rogers (1870–1957). Austin by Paul Barnes is a loose revival of the Bell type, closest to Austin's design in the two Text Roman versions, but with "the styling and sheen of New York in the 1970s" in the Regular and Hairline versions. It was originally designed for the British style magazine *Harper's & Queen*.

Detail of Eight Lines Pica from *A Specimen of Printing Types, by Edmund Fry and Co. Letter-Founders to the Prince of Wales* (London, 1787).

Big Moore | Isaac Moore (Edmund Fry, 1768) – Matthew Carter (Font Bureau, 2014)

ABCDEFGHIJKLMNOPQQRST
UVWXYZ&&abcdefghijklmnopqrst
uvwxyzⱥⱦⱨⱦⱨⱦⱦⱦⱦⱦⱦⱦ
1234567890{[(.,;:!?*)]}¶

Austin Text Roman | Richard Austin (1780s) – Paul Barnes (Commercial Type, 2007)

ABCDEFGHIJKKLMNOPQQQRRR
STUVWXYZ&ABCDEFGHIJKKLMNOP
QQRRRSTUVWXYZabcdefghijkklmnopq
rsttuvwxyzⱦfbffffhfifjfkflstffbffhffiffj
ffkffl12345678901234567890
{[(.,;:!?*)]}¶

COMPARISON: **Q**s from 1887 specimen of Bell's English Roman vs. Austin.

Neoclassical Types

The Didot family is usually credited with the invention of the types known in their time as the *goût nouveau* or modern style that is now described as neoclassical. The first of the types in this direction were cut by Pierre-Louis Wafflard (active 1781–1824) for Françoise-Ambroise Didot (1730–1804) in the early 1780s. But it is the work of Firmin Didot, son of Didot l'aîné, who cut his first type, a 12 pt italic, at the age of nineteen, that came to define the style. His romans first appear in *Essai de Fables Nouvelles* by La Fontaine (1786)—to which was appended a reprint of the 1784 *Épître sur les Progrès de l'Imprimérie* written by Didot fils l'aîné (Pierre Didot [1761–1853], Firmin's older brother)—as his father proudly announces on the title page. The letters have hairline serifs and vertical stress, but are light in weight.

Firmin designed letters with stronger stroke contrast in the 1790s for use in a series of sumptuous editions of the classics—Virgil (1798), Horace (1799), and Racine (1801–1805)—published by his brother Pierre. They represent the epitome of the neoclassical style, so-called because of their contemporaneity with the neo-classical revival of the Napoleonic era.

In Italy, Giambattista Bodoni was evolving types along the same lines as Firmin Didot at virtually the same time. He began his typographic career at the press of the Propaganda Fide, the missonary arm of the Vatican, in 1758 before being lured a decade later to Parma by Guillaume du Tillot (1711–1774), the French minister to Ferdinand, the Duke of Parma (1720–1765). At Parma, Bodoni took charge of the Stamperia Reale, where much of what he printed for the following four decades author Valerie Lester has aptly described as "sillinesses for the court—pamphlets, announcements, and little poems in celebration of little events."

At the outset of his career in Parma Bodoni used the types of Fournier. The first types that he cut and cast himself, shown in the 1771 *Fregi e Majuscole* specimen, were direct imitations of Fournier. But by the time he issued his magnificent *Manuale Tipografico* (in three formats) and *Serie di Majuscole e caratteri cancelleres-chi* in 1788, his types had undergone a major transformation, becoming modern like those of Firmin Didot, though more varied in design and warmer in feeling. Their first major appearance was in a Horace Bodoni printed after being permitted by the duke to set up his own imprint (Co' tipi Bodoniani) in 1791. It was the first

OPPOSITE: The punch for **R** (Maiuscole 101) cut by Giambattista Bodoni at the Museo Bodoniano (Parma). Photograph by Paul Shaw, 2008. See p. 4 for the other capital punches.

in a folio series of classics that rivaled those of the Didots. In 1818, after his death, Bodoni's widow and his foreman Luigi Orsi completed his magnum opus, a second *Manuale Tipografico* in two volumes (one devoted to Latin types and the other to Greek, Cyrillic, and exotic types).

The types of Didot and Bodoni, especially as they were refined in the 1790s, are characterized by capitals of nearly uniform width (with **R** having a curved leg), extreme stroke contrast with abrupt transitions from thick to thin, minimally bracketed (or in Didot's case, unbracketed) hairline serifs, and ball terminals. Their italics often have serifs in place of curled entry strokes in the lowercase. All of these features represent the influence of the pointed pen over the broad-edged nib and of letters incised into copperplates for engraving.

Beginning in the early 1790s and running well into the 19th century the work of Didot and Bodoni influenced printing and type design throughout Europe, including England and Scotland. In Germany, Johann Carl Ludwig Prillwitz (1759–1810) and Johann Friedrich Unger (1753–1804) argued over who was the first to cut letters in the new style, the former issuing a specimen of fourteen size of "neuer Didotscher Lettern" in 1790 and the latter showing his Neue Deutsche Lettern a year later. But it is the modern types of Justus Erich Walbaum (1768–1839), first shown c. 1803, that have been more influential than either of them.

Although affected by the new style, the English and Scottish founders never fully succumbed to its most extreme forms. The Shakespeare Printing Office, established in 1790 by George Nicol (c. 1740–1828) and John Boydell (1720–1800) and managed by William Bulmer (1757–1830) to print a nine-volume edition of Shakespeare (1792–1802), sought to match the magnificence of Bodoni's books. The type cut for it by William Martin shows the influence of both Baskerville and Bodoni. With new types cut by John Isaac Drury (fl. 1790–1820), even the venerable Caslon foundry succumbed to the new style in the 1790s. In Edinburgh, Richard Austin (1756–1832) cut types for the foundry of William Miller in 1822, since known as Scotch Modern or Scotch Roman, that are sturdier than those of Didot. Hairlines are not as brittle, serifs retain some bracketing, and the transition from thick to thin is less abrupt.

This chapter includes revivals of neoclassical types by Didot, Vibert, Bodoni, Walbaum, Austin, and John Isaac Drury.

OPPOSITE: Title page for the folio edition of *Quintus Horatius Flaccus* (Paris: Pierre Didot, 1799).

QUINTUS

HORATIUS

FLACCUS.

Lib. Franc.

PARISIIS,

IN AEDIBUS PALATINIS

SCIENTIARUM ET ARTIUM,

M. DCC. XCIX, REIP. VIII,

EXCUDEBAM PETRUS DIDOT, NATU MAJOR.

Bodoni

ni nella Toga e elle Armi. Ella mia dolcissima

Giambattista Bodoni may have been the most prolific punchcutter ever. The inventory of 1843 lists 25,491 punches. His second *Manuale Tipografico* (completed by his widow in 1818) contains 142 romans and italics. They vary in style (reflecting changes in influence from Fournier to Firmin Didot), width, weight, shape of curves, x-height, and serif structure. This abundance of Bodoni designs is at odds with the popular conception of what "Bodoni" should look like. The latter has been shaped by the mechanical forms of ATF Bodoni (1910) designed by Morris Fuller Benton, the first and most widespread revival of Bodoni, known digitally as Bodoni Book.

ITC Bodoni, with three optical sizes, is an attempt to create a truer Bodoni. Holly Goldsmith and Janice Prescott Fishman based the design of ITC Bodoni Seventy-Two on Bodoni's Papale, his largest type. Jim Parkinson (b.1941) created ITC Bodoni Six following smaller Bodoni designs such as the Nompariglia types. Sumner Stone (b.1945), who supervised the whole project, interpolated those two designs to achieve ITC Bodoni Twelve. He also designed the separate ITC Bodoni Seventy-Two Swash (1995).

Filosofia by Zuzana Licko is a personal interpretation of Bodoni's types with narrow proportions and deliberately thicker thin strokes. Despite its name it is not a direct revival of any of the ten types called Filosofia shown in the 1818 *Manuale Tipografico*. Note the ball terminals on the leg of **R** and the strokes of **s**; and the raised oldstyle figure **3**. Filosofia has a unicase companion inspired by the alphabet experiments of graphic designer Bradbury Thompson (1911–1995).

Detail of the Papale type from *Serie di Maiuscole e Carrateri Cancellareschi* by Giambattista Bodoni (Parma, 1788).

ITC Bodoni Seventy-Two Book and Ornaments | Giambattista Bodoni (Papale, 1788) – Janice Prescott Fishman and Holly Goldsmith (ITC, 1994)

ABCDEFGHIJKLMNOPQRSTUVWXY Z&ABCDEFGHIJKLMNOPQRSTUVWXYZ& abcdefghijklmnopqrstuvwxyzfifl 1234567890 1234567890{[(.,;:!?*)]}¶

ITC Bodoni Twelve Book | Giambattista Bodoni – Sumner Stone (ITC, 1994)

ABCDEFGHIJKLMNOPQRSTUVW XYZ&ABCDEFGHIJKLMNOPQRSTUVWXYZ &abcdefghijklmnopqrstuvwxyzfifl 1234567890 1234567890{[(.,;:!?*)]}

grandi :l Regno, bricat uta nella Emanuel Fi Abate Cesa . Vi risiede

Three types from *Serie di Maiuscole e Carrateri Cancellareschi* by Giambattista Bodoni (Parma, 1788): Imperiale | Corale grasso | Trismegisto grasso.

R R R

a a a

g g g

g g

Filosofia | Giambattista Bodoni (1788) – Zuzana Licko (Emigre, 1997)

ABCDEFGHIJKLMNOPQRSTUVWXYZ&
ABCDEFGHIJKLMNOPQRSTUVWXYZabcdefgh
ijklmnopqrstuvwxyzfifl1234567890
{[(.,;:!?*)]}¶ABCDEFGHIJKLMNOPQRSTU
VWXYZ&ABCDEFGHIJKLMNOPQRSTUVWXYZ
1234567890{[(.,;:!?*)]}¶ABCDEFGHIJKL
mnopqrstuvwxyz&1234567890
{[(.,;:!?*)]}¶

g st gst

2 2 2

COMPARISON (ABOVE): **g, s, t** from Trismegisto Sottile type by Bodoni vs. Filosofia.
COMPARISON (BELOW): Figures from Filosofia.

Didot

s Racine edi

typographic

forma, mox

The types of Firmin Didot continued to evolve over the course of his career, which began with the cutting of a 12 pt italic in 1783 and ended in the 1830s. Most noticeably, the contrast between thick and thin strokes became more and more pronounced. The types that he cut and cast for the spectacular "Editions du Louvre" series of the classics printed by his brother Pierre Didot are the epitome of the neoclassical style. They are the source for Linotype Didot by Adrian Frutiger (1928–2015) which has display and text versions that differ in the design of some characters as well as in weight and stroke contrast.

HTF Didot was designed by Jonathan Hoefler (b.1970) at the request of Fabien Baron, art director of *Harper's Bazaar*, as part of his attempt to recapture the spirit of the magazine's glory years under the direction of Alexey Brodovitch (1898–1971). It is based principally on the

Grosse Sans Pareille no. 206 cut by Joseph Molé le jeune—and shown by him at the "Exposition du Louvre" of 1819—that until recently was believed to have been the work of Firmin Didot; along with types by Didot shown in his brother Pierre's 1819 type specimen book. The HTF Didot family is notable for its seven optical sizes—including a 96 pt master—intended to preserve the delicate hairlines typical of Didot in headlines and larger situations. A more recent interpretation of Molé le jeune's version of Didot is Le Jeune (2013) by Paul Barnes and Christian Schwartz (b.1977), available in four optical sizes.

LP Didot by Garrett Boge is based on a 1784 design by the young Firmin Didot that was revived in 1926 by Ludwig & Mayer. It has less extreme stroke contrast than Linotype Didot or HTF Didot.

Detail from "Typographus Lectore" in *Quintus Horatius Flaccus* (Paris: Pierre Didot, 1799).

Linotype Didot Roman | Firmin Didot (1790s) – Adrian Frutiger (Linotype, 1991)

ABCDEFGHIJKLMNOPQRSTU
VWXYZ&ABCDEFGHIJKLMNOPQRSTU
vwxyz&abcdefghijklmnopqrstuvwx
yzfifl12345678901234567890
{[(.,;:!?*)]}¶

Ra Ra Ra

2222

COMPARISON (ABOVE): **R, a** from *Quintus Horatius Flaccus* vs. Linotype Didot Headline | Linotype Didot Roman.
COMPARISON (BELOW): **2** from Linotype Didot Headline | Linotype Didot Roman | HTF Didot L64 Light | LP Didot.

Linotype Didot Headline | HTF Didot L64 Light | LP Didot Display | Didot Elder

HTF Didot L42 | Firmin Didot and Molé le jeune – Jonathan Hoefler (Hoefler Type Foundry, 1992)

ABCDEFGHIJKLMNOPQRSTUVW
XYZ&abcdefghijklmnopqrstuvwxyz
ff fi fl ffi ffl 1234567890 {[(.,:;!?*)]} ◖

LP Didot | Firmin Didot (1784) – Garrett Boge (LetterPerfect, 1990)

ABCDEFGHIJKLMNOPQRSTUVWXY
Z&abcdefghijklmnopqrstuvwxyzffififlft
1234567890{[(.,:;!?*)]}¶

ABOVE (LEFT TO RIGHT): Three types by Firmin Didot: from "Notes" in *Épitre sur les Progrès l'Imprimerie* by Didot, fils Aîné (Paris, 1784), p. 20 | from "Avertissement" in *Essai de Fables Nouvelles…* by Françoise-Ambroise Didot (Paris, 1786) | from "Avertissement" in *Poésies* by Firmin Didot (Paris, 1834).

Vibert père

s de nos rois, dont les fils au

t de l'état sont l'espoir et l'a

e l'éclat de ton nom tutélair

e quelque orgueil cet œuvre

immortel qui du meilleur d

les Français éternise les dro

ros vaillant, humain, et ma

entier Voltaire a captivé l'e

Pierre Didot, Firmin's older brother, was a printer who established a foundry in the first decade of the 19th century with Joseph Vibert l'aîné (d. 1813) as its punchcutter. In his 1819 specimen book he announced that for over ten years (beginning sometime before 1803) he had personally supervised Vibert in the making of a series of new types, including being responsible for the unusual design of the **g** and **y**. The **g** has an open, seriffed lower bowl while the **y** has a vertical tail. The types have another unusual feature: arrow-shaped finials on **C**, **G**, **S**, **f**, **s** and **t**. This typeface was revived as Optimo Didot the Elder by François Rappo (b. 1955) in both display and text sizes.

Detail from p. 10 of *Specimen des Nouveaux Caractères de la Fonderie et de l'Imprimerie de P. Didot, L'Aîné* (Paris: Chez P. Didot, l'Ainé et Jules Didot, fils, 1819).

Optimo Didot the Elder Roman | Joseph Vibert l'aîné (Pierre Didot, 1819) – François Rappo (Optimo, 2004)

ABCDEFGHIJKLMNOPQRSTUV
WXYZ&abcdefghijklmnopqrstuvw
xyzfifl1234567890 1234567890
{[(.,;:!?*)]}¶

COMPARISON: **C**, **V**, **g**, **s**, **y** by Joesph Vibert l'aîné vs. Optimo Didot the Elder Roman.

Vibert fils

à l'angle de l'im-

de la rue Saint-

upés à l'angle de

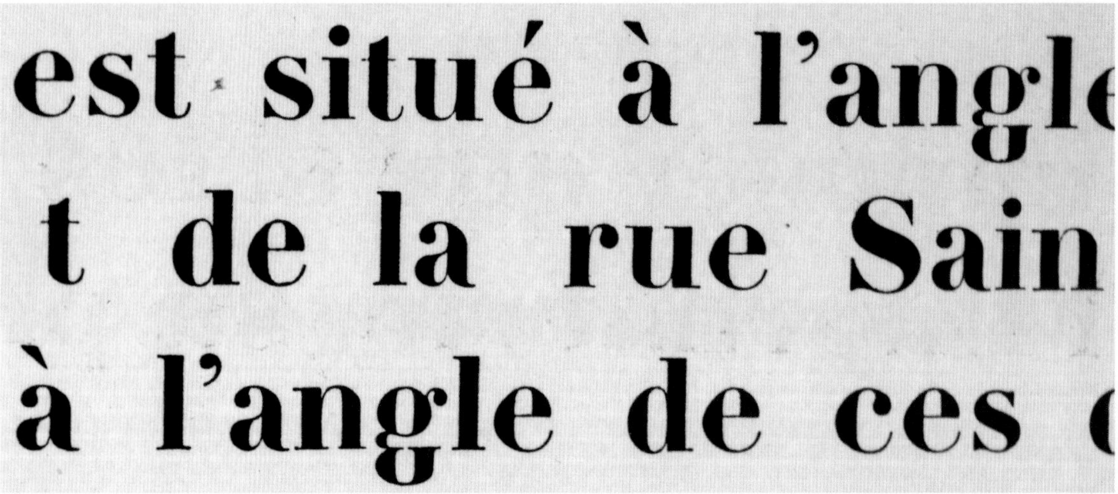

est · situé à l'angle

t de la rue Sain

à l'angle de ces d

Ambroise by Jean-François Porchez is attributable in part to types cut by Jean-Michel Vibert (1797–1862), known as Vibert fils, for Pierre Didot c. 1830. They have the same peculiar g and y as the types by Vibert l'aîné, but are bolder. Capitals with rounded extremities, based on types cut in the 1820s by Jules Didot (1794–1871), son of Pierre Didot, have been added to the character set as alternates, along with a single-story **a**, and a descending **f**. The **K** and **k** both have Cyrillic-looking curled arms with ball terminals. Even bolder (fat face) versions of the Vibert **g-y** types, known as Gras Vibert, were issued by the Deberny & Peignot foundry in the early 20th century.

Detail of Romain Gras Vibert from *Spécimen Général* (Paris: Fonderies Deberny & Peignot, c. 1926), Tome II, Division no. 5 "Classiques".

Ambroise with alternates | Jean-Michel Vibert (Pierre Didot, c. 1830) – Jean François Porchez
(Typofonderie Porchez, 2001)

AⱯBCDEⱸFGHIJK̶LMNⱤOPQRSTUV
WXYZ&aɑbcdeffgghiijk̶llmnopqrstuʋ
vwxyẙzɑffffififlffiffflstʧ1223456789oO
{[(.,:;:!?*)]}ꝓ

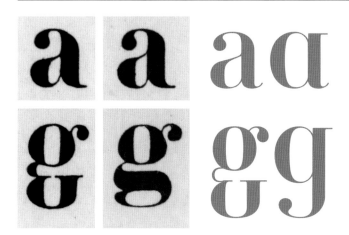

Qky

COMPARISON (ABOVE): Alternate forms of **a** and **g** from Gras Vibert specimen vs. Ambroise.
BELOW: Distinctive letters in Ambroise.

Walbaum

us Antiqua. a

nn, vornehmlich bei s

e Welt, wird gewöhnlich

urtheilt, mit der er ur

URTHEILEN ist völlig

h Anfangs nicht gan

n besten Gesellschaften 7

r es doch ganz in seine

llschaften zu vermeiden.

Justus Erich Walbaum acquired the foundry of the printer Ernst Wilhelm Kircher at Goslar in 1796. He moved it to Goslar in 1803, about the time he issued his first specimen of type. His Cicero Antiqua and Corpus Antiqua, influenced by the types of Firmin Didot, were original designs in the neoclassical manner. His letters are simpler than those of Didot and Bodoni and have stronger serifs. There are no spurs on the finial stroke serifs of **C**, **G** and **S**; the jaw of **G** is high, the curved leg of **R** ends flat, and the link of **g** juts out to the left.

Walbaum sold his business to F. A. Brockhaus in 1836 from whom H. Berthold acquired it in 1918. Berthold issued two versions of Walbaum, one light and spindly and the other robust with a larger x-height. Both were copied by the Monotype Corporation (c. 1932). Walbaum 10 by František Štorm follows the lighter design by Walbaum. Like other revivals by Štorm (see his Jannon [p. 67] and Baskerville [p. 95]) the type includes modern ligatures, several of which are strange (e.g., **offi**).

Detail of Corpus Antiqua from *Schriftproben aus der Giesserey von I.E. Walbaum in Goslar* (c. 1800).

Walbaum 10 Pro | Justus Erich Walbaum (c. 1800) – František Štorm (Storm Type Foundry, 2010)

ABCDEFGHIJKLMNOPQRST UVWXYZ&abcdefghijklmnopqrs tuvwxyzThTiWhctfbffffhfifjfkflftof sßpstffbffhffiffjffkfflfftoffofioffi 11223456789o1234567890 {[(.,;:!?*)]}¶

COMPARISON (ABOVE): **g**, **k** from Corpus Antiqua by Walbaum vs. Walbaum 10 Pro.
COMPARISON (BELOW): Monotype Walbaum vs. Berthold Walbaum Book.

Austin·Drury

Quousque
patientia n
furor iste t
sese effren
ne te noc

Quousque
nostra? q
det? quen
dacia? nil
nihil urbis

Several decades after cutting the Bell types (see pp. 104–105), Richard Austin (1756–1832) cut types for Alexander Wilson & Son in Glasgow and William Miller in Edinburgh. In 1819 he set up his own firm under the name of the Imperial Letter Foundry. In the preface to his first specimen he criticized the "modern or newfashioned faced printing type" as too fragile, "with hairlines so extremely thin as to render it impossible for them to preserve their delicacy beyond a few strokes of the lye-brush, or the most careful distribution." The types he made for the Scottish foundries avoided these faults. New Pica No. 2, cut for Miller in 1822, was sold as Scotch in the United States. A later Miller & Richard recasting (marred by badly recut sorts) became known as Scotch Roman, a standard book face in both England and the United States from the middle of the 19th century until the demise of metal type in the 1970s.

Miller by Matthew Carter (b. 1937) is a modernized version of Austin's types, capturing their essence while avoiding eccentricities such as the overly heavy capitals.

However, the **t** has a flat top. In keeping with Austin's views, the thin strokes of the Text version are strong. The Miller family has been extensively extended by various designers at the Font Bureau over the subsequent eighteen years.

Commercial Type describes the Brunel family by Paul Barnes and Christian Schwartz as "an English modern; an anthology of the late eighteenth and nineteenth century English foundries" drawn from several sources. Brunel Deck Roman is based on the New Pica Roman cut by John Isaac Drury in 1796 for Elizabeth Caslon, part of a reluctant but realistic attempt by the widow of Henry Caslon I to modernize the Caslon foundry's stock of type. Brunel Deck Roman No. 2 is a slightly heavier version. Both designs have alternate forms of **K, t, 2, 4, 7** and **8**.

Another recent interpretation of the Scotch types is Scotch Modern (2008) by Nick Shinn (b. 1952) which has a sans serif companion based on 19th-century grotesques.

LEFT: Detail of New Great Primer from *A Specimen of Modern Cut Printing Types, by Alex. Wilson & Sons, Letter Founders, Glasgow* (Glasgow, 1815).
RIGHT: Detail of Elizabeth Caslon's New Pica (1790s).

Miller Text | Richard Austin (Alexander Wilson, 1810) – Matthew Carter (Font Bureau, 1997)

ABCDEFGHIJKLMNOPQRRSTU
VWXYZ&&ABCDEFGHIJKLMNOPQ
RRSTUVWXYZ&abcdefghijklmnopqr
stuvwxyzff fi fj fl ffi ffl
1234567890{[(.,;:!?*)]}¶

Brunel Deck Roman | John Isaac Drury (1790s) – Paul Barnes with Christian Schwartz
(Commercial Type, 1995–2008)

ABCDEFGHIJKKLMNOPQRSTU
VWXYZ&ABCDEFGHIJKKLMNOPQRS
TUVWXYZ&abcdefghijklmnopqrsttu
vwxyzfbfffhfifjfkflftftffbffhffiffjffkffl
fftffft{[(.,;:!?*)]}¶11222334456778890

COMPARISON (LEFT): ts from New Great Primer by Austin vs. Austin Text.
COMPARISON (RIGHT): ts from New Pica by Drury vs. Brunel Deck Roman.

FRAN

dang

Mat

Fat Faces

The birthplace of the Industrial Revolution, England was the first country where the needs of commerce and the pressures of advertising affected type design. At the dawn of the 19th century, the design of types took a radical turn, becoming bolder and brasher as they were intended for use in trade cards, fliers, handbills, and posters rather than books.

The first of these new styles to appear was the fat face, shown c. 1803 in a specimen by Robert Thorne (d. 1820), owner of the Fann Street Foundry. The unflattering, though visually accurate, name comes from Thomas Hansard (1776–1833) who in his *Typographia* of 1825 unfavorably contrasted the new types with the existing "lean faces," referring to neoclassical types. In fact, the fat faces were essentially neoclassical types with their thick strokes pumped up, but their hairline strokes left intact—bastard offspring of book types intended for jobbing printing. They were much heavier than anything either Didot or Bodoni had achieved. And they were larger. In his 1825 specimen book, William Thorowgood (d. 1877), the successor to Thorne, showed a 24-line Pica (equivalent to 288 pts or nearly double the largest type of the 16th century, a 14 points de Cicéro). Until then book types had rarely been made in sizes larger than Gros Canon (44 pt).

Some fat faces became so bulked up that their counters were mere slits, such as the Four Lines Pica, No. 3 from Caslon & Livermore (1830). English printer William Savage (1770–1843) excoriated these extreme designs, writing in 1841 that, "We have types of beautiful shapes and symmetrical proportions, but our type founders have diverged, for the sake of variety, gradually to a fatter face till the lines have become so thick that the letter has hardly any white in its interior, and when printed is nearly all black, with the outline only to guide us in knowing what it is…."

Thorne's innovation was soon copied by William Caslon IV (1781–1869), Edmund Fry, Vincent Figgins (1766–1844), and other London typefounders. And from England it spread to the Continent and the United States where it was copied by wood type manufacturers as well as founders. Fat faces, along with egyptians and grotesques, became staple elements (both in metal and wood) of 19th-century broadsides.

This chapter shows two fat faces of differing weight and degree of stylization.

OPPOSITE: Detail of Eight Line Pica Roman and Italic from *Specimen of Plain and Ornamental Wood Type, Cut by Machinery by Wells & Webb, (Late D. Wells & Co.)* (New York: J.W. Oliver, 1840).

Figgins · Caslon IV

FIVE LINES PICA, No. 1.
DURHAM, Chelmsford. 123456789!
V. FIGGINS.

One of the most important and influential English type-foundries in the first half of the 19th century was that of Vincent Figgins (1766–1844). Figgins did not cut his own punches and the identity of who did is unknown. Among those shown in his 1815 specimen book are several fat faces that were part of a new trend toward types for advertising purposes. They inspired Matthew Carter to design a typeface called Elephant which has since been renamed Big Figgins. Like Carter's other "big" designs (see Big Caslon, p. 83 and Big Moore, p. 99), it is a synthesis of several sizes of type, principally Five Lines Pica and Four Lines Pica.

Isambard by Paul Barnes and Christian Schwartz is a bolder companion to their Brunel family (see p. 119).

It is based on several fat faces (e.g., Four Lines Pica, No. 3) cut in the 1820s and shown in the 1825 specimen of Caslon & Livermore. Isambard is darker than Big Figgins, with a larger x-height, smaller counters and more abrupt transitions from curve to straight. It contains both historical and modernized forms of **f** and **f**-ligatures.

ABOVE (TOP): Five Lines Pica, No. 1 from *Specimen of Printing Types, by Vincent Figgins, Letter-Founder* (London, 1815).
COMPARISON (RIGHT): **a** from Four Lines Pica, No. 3 specimen by Caslon & Livermore (1825) vs. Isambard.

Big Figgine [Elephant] | Four Lines Pica (Vincent Figgins, 1815) – Matthew Carter (Carter & Cone, 1992)

ABCDEFGHIJKLMNOPQR
STUVWXYZ&abcdefghijklmn
opqrstuvwxyz ff fi fj fl ffi ffl
1234567890{[(.,;:!?*)]}¶

Isambard | Four Lines Pica, No. 3 (Caslon & Livermore, 1820) – Paul Barnes with Christian Schwartz
(Commercial Type, 1995–2008)

ABCDEFGHIJKLMNOP
QRSTUVWXYZ&abcdeff
ghijklmnopqrstuvwxyz
fb ff ff fh fi fj fk fl ft ffb ffi ffj ffk
ffl fft 1234567890
{[(.,;:!?*)]}¶

COMPARISON: Big Figgins vs. Isambard.

Caslon IV

LIDEN
BOND WARE
BONAPARTE

One of the oddest typefaces ever designed in the metal era is the so-called Caslon Italian, a fat face that has been turned inside out with thins becoming thick and vice versa. It first appeared in an 1821 specimen issued by Caslon & Catherwood. The design spread rapidly, copied first by founders in England, Europe, and the United States; and then by the new breed of wood type manufacturers. It was issued in a wide range of sizes from 2-line Pica to 12-line Pica. There were subtle differences among several of the versions of Italian, most noticeable in the treatment of the leg of **R**.

Originally designed for use in *The New York Times Magazine*, Arbor is a modern take on Caslon Italian by Chester Jenkins (b. 1971) that is visually smoother than the original. The widths have been standardized; the heavy triangular serifs at the end of horizontal strokes in **E**, **F**, **L** and **T** have been abandoned; and the ball terminal found on the leg of **R** in some versions has become a motif throughout the face. Furthermore, there is a lowercase, something which William Caslon IV did

not cut, but which is found in later versions such as the Italienische Antiqua-Schriften shown by the German foundry of E. Haenel in 1845.

A more faithful version of the Caslon IV design, though not in all respects (see the inventive **Q**), is Caslon Italian (2005) by Paul Barnes, while a tongue-in-cheek interpretation is Karloff Negative, the dark alter-ego to Karloff Positive. Karloff (2012) by Peter Bil'ak (b. 1973), Pieter van Rosmalen (b. 1969), and Nikola Djurek (b. 1976) explores "the idea of irreconcilable differences."

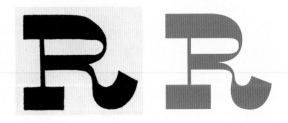

TOP: Detail of 10- and 5-line Pica Italian, and 7-line Pica Gothic Italian from *Specimen of Plain and Ornamental Wood Type, Cut by Machinery by Wells & Webb, (Late D. Wells & Co.)* (New York: J.W. Oliver, 1840).
COMPARISON (ABOVE RIGHT): **R** from 1821 Caslon Italian vs. Caslon Italian (Commercial Type).

Arbor | Italian (William Caslon IV, 1821) – Chester Jenkins (Village, 2008 / 2010)

ABCDEFGHIJKLMNOPQRST
UVWXYZ&abcdefghijklmnopqr
stuvwxyz1123456789O
{[(.,;:!?*)]}¶

Caslon Italian | Italian (William Caslon IV, 1821) – Paul Barnes (Commercial Type, 2005)

ABCDEFGHIJKLMNOPQ&Q
R.RSTUVWXYZ&&aaabbcc
defgghijklmnopqqrstuvwxyz
1234567890[(.,;:!?*)]¶

COMPARISON: **R**, **k** from 5-line Pica Italian (Wells & Webb) vs. Caslon Italian (Commercial Type).

The **WM. H. PAGE WOOD TYPE Co.,**
NORWICH, CONN.

Ten Line No. 117.   Class C.   9 Cents.

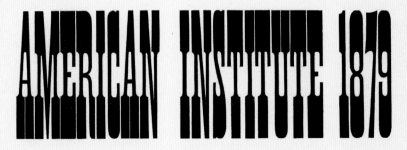

Border No. 203. $1,00 per foot.

Sixteen Line No. 117.   C. 12 Cents.

Border No. 202. $1,50 per foot.   (Patent pending.)

Slab Serifs

The next step in the attempt to make types bolder for advertising purposes occurred with the invention of the antique design, first shown in the 1815 specimen book of Vincent Figgins (1766–1844), in which all strokes of a letter were thickened equally—including the serifs. The antiques were attacked in William Savage's *Dictionary of the Art of Printing* (1841) as barbarous for their overly thick strokes and correspondingly thin negative spaces. Nevertheless, like the fat faces, they prospered with every founder in England, and then in Europe, with the United States making their own version.

In William Thorowgood's 1821 specimen book, antique designs were called egyptians, a name presumably derived from continuing excitement over egyptian antiquities engendered by Napoleon's campaign of 1798–1799, but also one that helped differentiate the slab serif design from sans serif faces that were also called antiques by some founders. The name egyptian stuck and is in common use today.

Egyptians spawned several distinctive slab serif variants. The first to appear, sometime in the early 1830s, was the ionic. It is distinguished by increased stroke contrast and slightly bracketed serifs. In 1845 Benjamin Fox (d. 1877) cut for the Fann Street Foundry (run at that point by Robert Besley [1794–1876]), a smaller and lighter form of the egyptian intended for use in dictionaries. Named Clarendon, it was the first type to be patented. The Clarendon name was subsequently appended to other slab serif designs that had nothing in common with Fox's type, most notably the French Clarendon, a condensed, reverse-weight style popular with wood type manufacturers.

Although closely associated with the American Wild West through their ubiquity on "Wanted" posters and other ephemera of the latter half of the 19th century, slab serif types were used by Dadaists for the mastheads of *Bulletin Dada* (1920), *Der Dada* (1920), and *Le Coeur de Barbe* (1922), and by artists like Victor Moscoso (b. 1936) for psychedelic posters in the 1960s.

OPPOSITE: Ten Line No. 117 and Sixteen Line No. 117 by The Wm. H. Page Wood Type Co. from *Page's Wood Type Album* (1879).

Nebiolo

Pedro González - Mendoza
Los mártires del Trabajo
7 BOMBITA QUINITO 8

Vaccination à Rome
Discours socialistes
9 - DÉCORATION - 2

Grande Lotteria
Libertà e Ordine
3 CONCERTO 4

Novellista
MARINAI

Tiratori

Patrie

Sebastian

Egiziano Nero first appears in a Nebiolo type specimen in 1920 under the name Tondo Nero Normale as part of the Egizianio Serie 302. The design was supposedly electrotyped from Stevens Shanks Antique No. 6, which was originally an egyptian shown by Figgins in 1815. Like many foundry types, some of its letters vary considerably in form from size to size.

In the 1970s Roger Black (b. 1948), art director at *Rolling Stone* magazine, discovered Egiziano Nero and it became one of his favorite typefaces. Dennis Ortiz-Lopez (b. 1949), a lettering artist who often worked for the music magazine, has digitized the Nebiolo design as OL Egiziano Classic, basing it on the Corpo 24 size. OL Egiziano Classic Black, like its model, has a larger x-height than the Figgins original and more consistent distribution of weight.

Jim Parkinson has made an interpretation of Egiziano Nero as Sutro Heavy (2003).

Egiziano (Serie 302) Tondo Nero Normale from *Campionario, Caratteri e Fregi Tipografici* (Torino: Ditta Nebiolo & Comp., 1920), p. 317.

OL Egiziano Classic Black | Egiziano Nero (Nebiolo, 1920) electrotyped from Stevens Shanks Antique No. 6 – Dennis Ortiz-Lopez (OL Fonts, 2003)

ABCDEFGHIJKLMNOPQ QRSTUVWXYZ&abcdefghi jklmnopqrstuvwxyzfifl 1234567890{[(.,;:!?*)]}¶

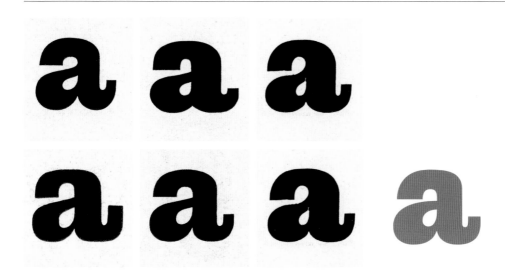

COMPARISON: Egiziano **a** at different point sizes (Corpo 16, Corpo 20, Corpo 24, Corpo 32, Corpo 36, and Corpo 48) vs. OL Egiziano Classic Black.

Spencer

Over the past decade and a half Eric Kindel, on the faculty of the Department of Typography and Communication at the University of Reading, has done extensive research into the history of stencils. Among his discoveries has been the work of S. M. Spencer (1842–1923) of Brattleboro, Vermont (later Boston), a manufacturer of stencilling kits. Fred Smeijers, with the input of Kindel, has created Puncho based on Spencer's alphabet for his 1-S Inch Forward Slant or Outfit Dies that was supplied with his "Twenty Five Dollar Outfit". He has given the letters a greater slant than they originally had, but otherwise left them as they were.

Puncho is part of the Stencil Fonts Series, a set of historically-based stencil designs from OurType that accompanied the 2012 exhibition *Between Writing & Type: The Stencil Letter* curated by Kindel and Smeijers. The others are Orly Stencil and Couteau by Pierre Pané-Farré (b. 1984), and Bery Roman and Bery Script by Smeijers. Another stencil font inspired by a different set of Spencer punches is Brattleboro Stencil JNL (2015) from Jeff Levine.

Puncho | S.M. Spencer (1860s) – Fred Smeijers (OurType, 2012)

ABCDEFGHIJKLMNOPQRST UVWXYZ&abcdefghijklm nopqrstuvwxyz1234567890 .,;:!?

OPPOSITE (LEFT): Copyrighted stencil designs and sample plates from the *Celebrated Improved Stencil Works of S. M. Spencer & Co., Brattleboro, Vt.* (n.d.). OPPOSITE (RIGHT): Fannie Fern stencil plate.
THIS PAGE (ABOVE): Detail of punches by S.M. Spencer (c. 1860–1900). Photograph by Ray Miller. THIS PAGE (BELOW): Equivalent letters from Puncho. Note the difference in slope.

Wood Type

For most of the first three and a half centuries of printing, from Gutenberg to Bodoni, type was larger than 60 pt. This was due to practical as well as aesthetic considerations. Larger sizes were more difficult to cast from matrices using a handmould. Instead, they were sometimes cast from leaden matrices struck with brass punches or, more commonly, cast in moulds of sand, plaster, or typemetal formed from patterns of wood or brass. Letters made in this latter manner were called dabs, clichés or *abklatschen*. For printing they were nailed to a wooden base. Thomas Cottrell (d.1785), dismissed for insubordination from the Caslon foundry in 1757, made letters equal to 12 lines of Pica in height for printing posters using the sandcasting process. They were shown in his specimen of 1765.

Along with the practical difficulties in making large types using the handmould, printers had little use for them, beyond title pages and initials. Types were cut and cast for use in books at text sizes, with more energy and ingenuity being expended on achieving small sizes than on large ones. Initials were cut in wood or engraved in metal (which was then mounted on wood); title pages were cut entirely in wood or later engraved in copper. In short, there was little aesthetic incentive to make large types until the advent of jobbing printing in the early 19th century.

At first the large sizes of the new fat faces, egyptians, and grotesques (the English name for sans serifs) were cast in moulds. Printers often found such types to be expensive, heavy, and brittle. In 1828, following experiments with a lateral router, Darius Wells (1800–1875) of Albany, New York produced the first specimen of wood type. This was the first significant change in the technology and material of type-making. The American wood type industry that sprang up in the wake of Wells' innovation initially took its designs from English typefounders. Thus, the first wood types were fat faces, egyptians, gothics (the American name for sans serifs), Tuscans (types with bifurcated serifs), and grecians (slab serifs with chamfered corners).

The making of wood type changed significantly after William Leavenworth (1799–1860) of Connecticut combined the router with a pantograph in 1834. His innovation allowed many sizes of type to be made from a single master design. More significantly (though not universally lauded), the use of the pantograph

OPPOSITE: Detail of Tuscan Extended wood type. Photograph from Hamilton Wood Type Museum.

GO AND SEE
THE WONDER of the AGE
A MAMMOTH
HEIFER

NOT SIX YEARS OLD,
WEIGHING 3400 POUNDS
NOW ON EXHIBITION
AT THE
WM. PENN HOTEL

Market Street, West Philadelphia.

FED BY ANTHONY BENDER, CHESTER CO.

ADMISSION ONLY 15 CENTS.

Quinn Card & Job Printer, S. W. cor. of Third & Market Sts. Philada.

also made it possible to alter the proportions of a design, condensing or enlarging them. Furthermore, as Rob Roy Kelly (1925–2004) has shown, the basic styles of wood type could be altered to spawn hybrids with compound names such as Antique Tuscan and Gothic Tuscan. American wood type manufacturers also copied the English foundries in making decorative extensions of the basic styles by adding contours, outlines, inlines, shading, shadows, and a variety of ornamental motifs. Wood type, like the large foundry type that preceded it, was measured in lines with some sizes being 100 lines in height or more. Since wood type was usually destined for use on broadsides, fonts frequently lacked lowercase letters.

Chromatic types, composed of two parts which could be inked in separate colors, were first shown by George Nesbitt (1808–1869) in 1841. However, it was William H. Page (1829–1906) whose name became synonymous with them upon the publication of his magnificent specimen book of 1874. His book marked the height of the wood type era. Competition became fiercer in the 1880s and in 1891 Page was bought by the Hamilton Mfg. Co., noted for its veneer wood type. Hamilton subsequently purchased Heber Wells in 1898, Morgans and Wilcox the following year, and the Tubbs Company in 1918, leaving it with a monopoly.

Before the ascendancy of Hamilton, wood type manufacturers, like their foundry counterparts, copied each other's designs, making it difficult to assign priority to one company over another in determining who originated a new style. Furthermore, many of the styles were imitations of typefaces produced by foundries in the United States, England, and France. However, despite the rampant copying, some subtle differences between apparently similar designs can often be found, as will be seen in this chapter.

A lightface and two fat faces, an egyptian, two grecians, three Tuscans of amazing diversity, a gothic Tuscan, a grotesque, and three chromatics are shown in this chapter, covering the essential categories of wood type styles. The French Clarendon style, associated so closely with images of the American Wild West, is not discussed (but an example can be seen on p. 126).

OPPOSITE: "The Wonder of the Age." A broadside printed by Quinn, Card & Job Printers (Philadelphia, c. 1865–1874).

Roman Ext.

A B C D
E F G H
I J K L
M N O P
Q R S T

HWT Roman Extended Fatface by Jim Lyles (b. 1955) is derived from Roman Extended, a 6-line sized type cut by Edwin Allen (1811–1891) of Norwich, Connecticut who sold his designs through George Nesbitt, a New York City printer. The design, which followed one cast in metal by Caslon in 1835, was first shown in George Nesbitt's *First Premium Wood Types: Cut by Machinery* (1838). The design was subsequently issued by other wood type manufacturers, including William H. Page, who produced his version between 1857 and 1859. The Page version is the basis for Madrone by Barbara Lind. See p. 231, *American Wood Type 1828–1900*.

There are subtle differences between HWT Roman Extended Fatface and Madrone such as the treatment of ball/lobe terminals and the design of figures **2, 5** and **7**. HWT Roman Extended Fatface also has more regularized alternate versions of **K, R, g** and **s**. A "companion" design to Roman Extended is Roman Extended Lightface (No. 251) by William H. Page (1872). Miranda Roth (b. 1990) has revived it as HWT Roman Extended Lightface (2012).

Detail of Roman Extended first shown by George Nesbitt (1838). From *American Wood Type 1828–1900* by Rob Roy Kelly (New York: Van Nostrand Reinhold Company, 1969), p. 231.

HWT Roman Extended Fatface | Roman Extended (Edwin Allen, 1838) – Jim Lyles (Hamilton WoodType, 2013)

ABCDEFGHIJK
KLMNOPQRRS
TUVWWXYZ&
abcdefgghijkl
mnopqrsstuvw
xyzffffifflffifffl
1234567890
{[(.,;:!?*)]}

Madrone | Roman Extended (Edwin Allen, 1838) – Barbara Lind (Adobe, 1991)

ABCDEFGHIJ
KLMNOPQRS
TUVWXYZ&ab
cdefghijklmn
opqrstuvwxyz
fifl1234567890
{[(-,;:!?*)]}

Antique

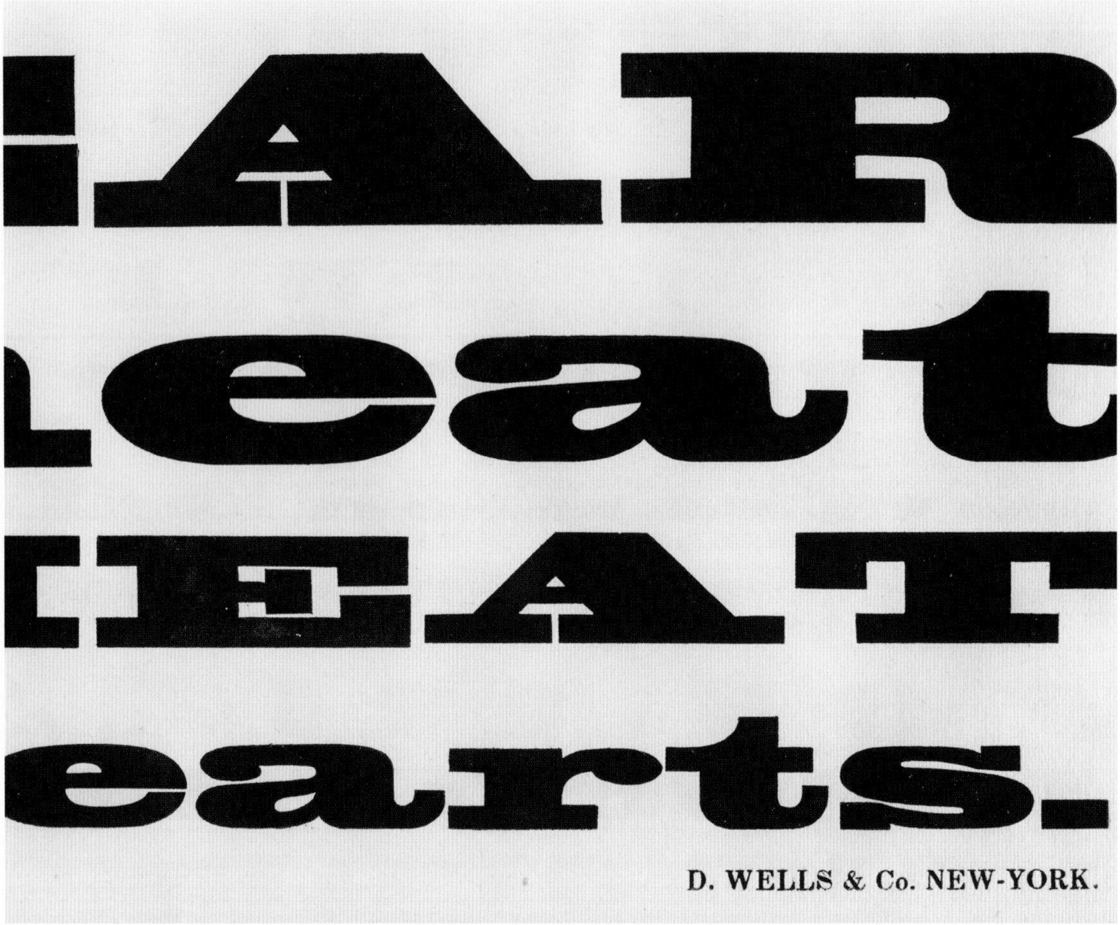

I AR
leat
EAT
earts.

D. WELLS & Co. NEW-YORK.

Despite its name, Antique Extended, first shown by Edwin Allen in a 4-line size in George Nesbitt's *First Premium Wood Types: Cut by Machinery* (1838), is an Egyptian. It is believed to be an original American design that was copied later by the typefounders as well as by other wood type manufacturers. It is unclear which version of Antique Extended is the basis for Blackoak by Joy Redick since there are significant differences between it and the one by Allen (e.g. **E**, **R**, **c** and **e**). The Rob Roy Kelly American Wood Type Collection at the University of Texas has Antique Extended (No. 254) by William H. Page and a 10-line Antique Extended from the Hamilton Mfg. Co. (see *American Wood Type 1828–1900*, p. 245) but neither has a lowercase.

Blackoak is part of the Adobe Wood Type 2 set with Birch, Madrone (pp. 136–137), Poplar (p. 155), and Willow.

Detail of 6- and 4-line Antique Extended from *Specimen of Plain and Ornamental Wood Type, Cut by Machinery by Wells & Webb (Late D. Wells & Co.)* (New York: J. W. Oliver, 1840).

Blackoak | Antique Extended (Edwin Allen, 1838) – Joy Redick (Adobe, 1991)

ABCDEFGHI
JKLMNOPQ
RSTUVWXY
Z&abcdefghi
jklmnopqrst
uvwxyzfifl
1234567890
{[(.,;:!?*)]}

COMPARISON: **A, E** from 4-line Antique Extended (Wells & Webb) vs. Blackoak.

GRECIAN

ABCDE
FGHIJ
KLMN

Grecian types are essentially egyptians with corners and extremities that have been chamfered. The first wood type designed in this manner—including chamfered serifs—is an 18-line Pica Antique Condensed, Cornered shown in George Nesbitt's 1838 specimen book (*American Wood Type 1828–1900*, p. 96). This design—not considered a grecian since it has curves—was copied from French typefounders and precedes the first grecians from English typefounders which are dated to the early 1840s. The first grecian shown by an American founder was from L. Johnson & Company in 1841; and the first by a wood type manufacturer was from Wells & Webb in 1846—both were extra condensed. The latter were the first to make a condensed variation in 1849. Ten years later William H. Page became the first to make a full face.

Acropolis by Jonathan Hoefler (b. 1970), part of The Proteus Project quartet of typefaces, is derived from Page's Full Faced Grecian (shown in *American Wood Type 1828–1900*, p. 275). Acropolis deviates from Page's design in several details: the counter of **C** is larger, the midstroke of **E** and **F** is thinner, the hook of **J** is angled, the middle of the spine of **S** is thinner, etc. But most importantly, Acropolis has an italic, something not found in any 19th century grecian.

OL Grecian Classic Bold Extra Condensed by Dennis Ortiz-Lopez differs in several details from Grecian Extra Condensed (1846) by Wells & Webb (*American Wood Type 1828–1900*, p. 276). There is no spur on the **G**, the middle of the spine of **S** is thinner, the counter of **U** is not chamfered. All of the figures are more consistently designed than those by Wells & Webb.

Acropolis | Full Faced Grecian (William Page, 1872) – Jonathan Hoefler (Hoefler Type Foundry, 1990)

ABCDEFGHIJKLMNOPQR
STUVWXYZ&abcdefghijkl
mnopqrstuvwxyzffffflftffi
ffl1234567890{[(.,:;!?*)]}¶

OL Grecian Classic Bold Extra Condensed | Grecian Extra Condensed (Wells & Webb, 1846) – Dennis Ortiz-Lopez (Dennis Ortiz-Lopez Typography, 2003)

ABCDEFGHIJKLMNOPQRST
UVWXYZ&1234567890[.,:;!?*)

OPPOSITE: Detail of Full Faced Grecian first shown by William Page (1859). From *American Wood Type 1828–1900* by Rob Roy Kelly (New York: Van Nostrand Reinhold Company, 1969), p. 275.
COMPARISON (ABOVE LEFT): **B** from Full Faced Grecian vs. Acropolis. (ABOVE RIGHT): **E** from Grecian Extra Condensed vs. OL Grecian Classic Bold Extra Condensed.

TUSCAN

Demented

ISTHMUS

10 Line Egyptian Ornamented.   D.   11 Cents.

REDER

AI Wood Tuscan Egyptian | Egyptian Ornamented (William H. Page, 1859) – Peter Fraterdeus (Alphabets, 1993)

ABCDEFGHIJKLMNOPQRSTUV
WXYZ&1234567890([(.,;:!?*)])

Egyptian Ornamented by William H. Page, first listed in his 1870 specimen, is the model for AI Wood Tuscan Egyptian by Peter Fraterdeus (b. 1954). Fraterdeus has called it a Tuscan Egyptian because the letters have bifurcated slab serifs. The decorative median spurs are typical of this style of type. This is the typeface often used on "Wanted" posters in the American West in the late 19th century. Although Page includes a lowercase in his 1872 specimen, AI Tuscan Egyptian only has capitals.

American Wood Type 1828–1900, p. 292 shows Egyptian Ornamented by the Tubbs Co., which is subtly different from the Page design: note the **A** and **K**. Tuscan Egyptian Thin (2005)—not shown here—by Jordan Davies (b. 1941) of Wooden Types based on Tuscan Egyptian (1880) from the Hamilton Mfg. Co. (*American Wood Type 1828–1900*, p. 293) is even more different. It is squatter; and has **A** with a forked crossbar and **Q** with an internal tail. More significantly, it has a lowercase.

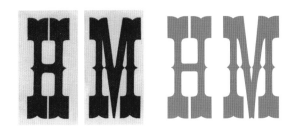

OPPOSITE: Detail of 10 Line Egyptian Ornamented from *Specimens of Wood Type Manufactured by Wm. H. Page & Co.* (Greeneville, Connecticut, 1872).
COMPARISON (ABOVE): **H**, **M** from 10 Line Egyptian Ornamented vs. AI Wood Tuscan Egyptian.

5 Line Tuscan Extended.   A.   7 Cents.

Detail of 4 Line and 5 Line Tuscan Extended from *Specimens of Wood Type Manufactured by Wm. H. Page & Co.* (Greeneville, Connecticut, 1872).

One of the more unusual variations on the Tuscan theme of bifurcated serifs by the wood type manufacturers—and there are several—is Tuscan Extended by William H. Page, extensively shown in his 1872 specimen but only briefly mentioned in *American Wood Type 1828–1900*. The letters, including the serifs, have low stroke contrast and the median decorative element is a simple horizontal bar (with the exception of **S** and **s**). Unlike most Tuscans, it has a lowercase. Frank Grieshammer (b. 1983), attracted by its weirdness, chose it as his contribution to the Hamilton Wood Type Collection of digital wood type revivals. He redrew the curves, making the letters even more monotone, and added many of the lowercase characters not present in printed examples of Page's type. The pilcrow is also a Grieshammer invention.

HWT Tuscan Extended | Tuscan Extended (William Page, 1872) – Frank Grieshammer
(Hamilton Wood Type, 2013)

ABCDEFGHIJKLMN
OPQRSTUVWXYZ&
abcdefghijklmnopqrst
uvwxyz{[(.,:;!?*)]}¶
1234567890

COMPARISON (TOP LINE): Tuscan Extended **N** in wood, printed and from HWT Tuscan Extended.
COMPARISON (BOTTOM LINE): **t** from Tuscan Extended vs. HWT Tuscan Extended. (BOTTOM RIGHT): HWT Tuscan Extended letters by Frank Grieshammer.

EIGHT LINES PICA GOTHIC TUSCAN ITALIAN.

MARKET

TEN LINES PICA GOTHIC TUSCAN ITALIAN.

GENIUS

TWELVE LINES PICA GOTHIC TUSCAN ITALIAN.

CHILD

SIXTEEN LINES PICA GOTHIC TUSCAN ITALIAN.

LION

WELLS & WEBB.   NEW YORK.

Eight Lines Pica, etc. Gothic Tuscan Italian from *Specimens of Wood Type, Manufactured by Wells & Webb…* (New York: 1854).

Cottonwood | Gothic Tuscan Italian (Wells & Webb, 1854) – Kim Buker Chansler, Barbara Lind and Joy Redick (Adobe, 1991)

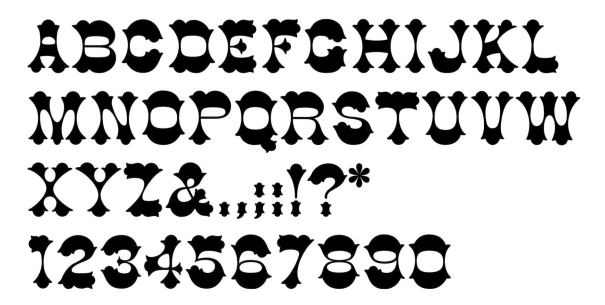

Darius Wells, the first man to manufacture wood type, took his employee Ebenezer Russell Webb (1811–1864) as a partner in 1839. One extant copy of their 1854 catalogue entitled *Specimens of Wood Type Manufactured by Wells & Webb* includes an unusual typeface called Gothic Tuscan Italian (see *American Wood Type 1828–1900*, p. 318.) The compound name is as odd as the design. It has no gothic elements and the only possible Italian aspect is the reversal of weight normally associated with a French Antique. The Tuscan part of the name is clearer since some strokes are bifurcated and the serifs, marked by the presence of lunettes, could be considered trifurcated. Some of the letters are remarkable for their figure/ground relationships.

Cottonwood, by the team of Kim Buker Chansler, Barbara Lind and Joy Redick, is a fairly straightforward rendition of Gothic Tuscan Italian. Only a few changes have been made: the tail of **Q** and part of the ampersand have been redesigned and a question mark added to the limited punctuation set. There was never a lowercase for this design. It was subsequently cast in small sizes by the typefounders.

Cottonwood is part of the Adobe Wood Type 1 set along with Ironwood (p. 149), Juniper, Mesquite (p. 149), and Ponderosa.

COMPARISON: **Q** from Gothic Tuscan Italian vs. Cottonwood.

ABCDEFGHIJ

KLMNOPQRS

TUVWXYZ&!

Both Mesquite and Ironwood by Joy Redick reflect the wild inventiveness of American wood type manufacturers. They are two more semi-ornamental extensions of the Tuscan concept. Mesquite is a revival of Antique Tuscan No. 8 (1859) from William H. Page, while Ironwood is a revival of Gothic Tuscan Pointed (1859) from John Cooley (1819–1909)—see *American Wood Type 1828–1900*, pp. 295 and 319 respectively. (Page's Antique Tuscan No. 10 [1859] is slightly wider than Cooley's design and has more consistently designed "points." More significantly, it has a lowercase.)

Mesquite is not identical to Antique Tuscan No. 8. Some of the counters have been opened up (see especially **C** and **G**), the spiky serifs have been regularized, and tail of the **Q** is different. The ampersand, figures, and some of the punctuation appear to be designed from scratch. A number of Ironwood characters differ from the Cooley design (and the Page version as well): **Q**, **&**, **4**, **5**, **7**. Where did they come from?

Mesquite and Ironwood are part of the Adobe Wood Type 1 set with Cottonwood (p. 147), Juniper, and Ponderosa.

Mesquite | Antique Tuscan No. 8 (William Page, 1859) – Joy Redick (Adobe, 1990)

ABCDEFGHIJKLMNOPQRSTUVWXYZ&
1234567890{[(.,;:!? *)]}

Ironwood | Gothic Tuscan Pointed (John Cooley, 1850) – Joy Redick (Adobe, 1990)

ABCDEFGHIJKLMNOPQRSTUVW
XYZ&1234567890{[(.,;:!?*)]}

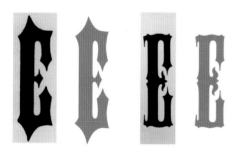

OPPOSITE: Detail of Gothic Tuscan Pointed first shown by both William Page and John Cooley (1859). From *American Wood Type 1828–1900* by Rob Roy Kelly (New York: Van Nostrand Reinhold Company, 1969), p. 319.
COMPARISON (ABOVE): **E** from Gothic Tuscan Pointed vs. Ironwood. (ABOVE RIGHT): **E** from Antique Tuscan No. 8 vs. Mesquite.

CHROMATICS

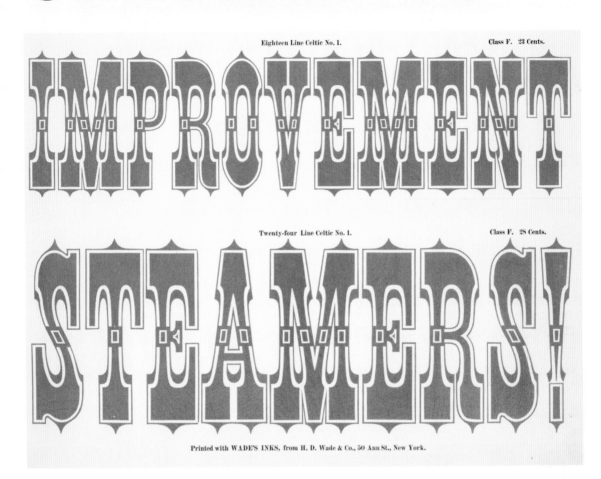

Eighteen Line Celtic No. 1.   Class F. 23 Cents.

Twenty-four Line Celtic No. 1.   Class F. 28 Cents.

Printed with WADE'S INKS, from H. D. Wade & Co., 50 Ann St., New York.

William H. Page is most renowned for his chromatic types, first shown at the back of his 1859 specimen, but then displayed spectacularly (thanks in part to the use of inks from H. D. Wade & Co.) in a large catalogue from 1874. Chromatic types are designed with multiple layers that can be inked separately and then combined to achieve decorative effects. The three types that comprise the Adobe Wood Type 3 set, designed by the team of Kim Buker Chansler, Carl Crossgrove and Carol Twombly, are ostensibly derived from designs in Page's 1874 catalogue: Pepperwood from Celtic No. 1 (1870; originally called Celtic Ornamented), Rosewood from Clarendon Ornamented (1859), and Zebrawood from Doric (1859).

However, close inspection reveals that all three differ in details, suggesting that the Adobe team relied on several sources for their designs; or that they made changes to adapt the typefaces for use at sizes much smaller than wood type. Pepperwood is squatter than Celtic No. 1 with pinchier counters and weaker shading. Rosewood (not shown here) is wider than Page's Clarendon Ornamented and some of the elongated diamond decorations are shaped differently. And Zebrawood has a decorative dot pattern that more closely matches the doric found in the 1854 Wells & Webb specimen than the one shown by Page.

Like Page's chromatic types, the Adobe designs are made in two parts, an outline and a fill.

Detail of Celtic No. 1 from *Specimens of Chromatic Wood Type, Borders, &c. Manufactured by Wm. H. Page & Co.* (Greeneville, Connecticut: Wm. H. Page & Co., 1874).

Pepperwood | Kim Buker Chansler, Carl Crossgrove and Carol Twombly (Adobe, 1994)

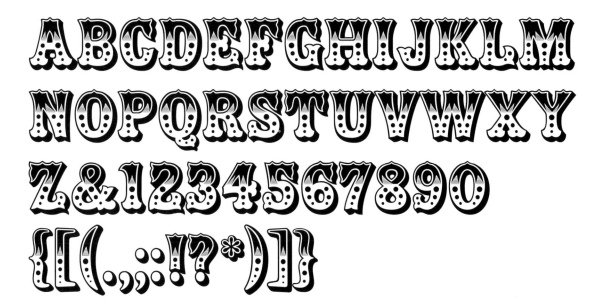

Zebrawood | Doric (Wells & Webb, 1854) – Kim Buker Chansler, Carl Crossgrove and Carol Twombly (Adobe, 1994)

COMPARISON (LEFT): **M** from Celtic No. 1 vs. Pepperwood.
COMPARISON (RIGHT): **R** from Twelve Line Pica Doric Ornamented (Wells & Webb, 1854) vs. Zebrawood.

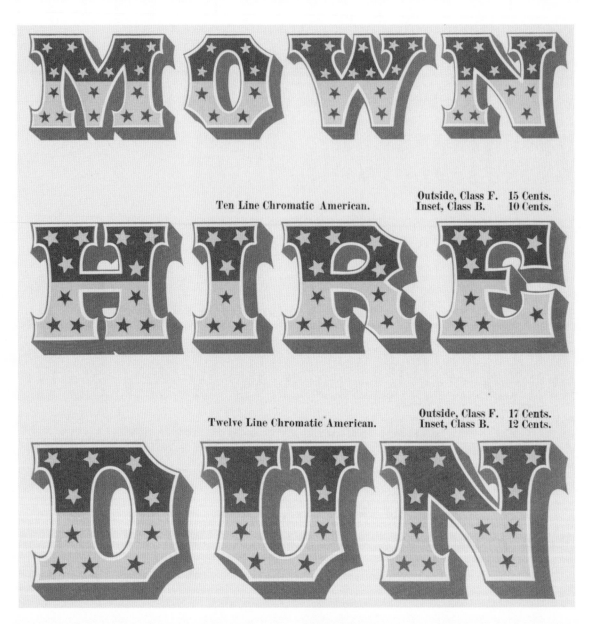

Ten Line Chromatic American.

Outside, Class F. 15 Cents.
Inset, Class B. 10 Cents.

Twelve Line Chromatic American.

Outside, Class F. 17 Cents.
Inset, Class B. 12 Cents.

HWT American Chromatic by Richard Kegler (b. 1965) and Terry Wudenbachs (b. 1970) is another typeface derived from W. H. Page & Co.'s celebrated 1874 catalogue of chromatic types. (See pp. 150–151.) It is a revival of Chromatic American (previously called American in Page's 1859 specimen). It is closer to its model than the Adobe chromatic trio are to theirs, though the decorative stars have been regularized and in several letters more evenly distributed (e.g., **D** and **U**). HWT American Chromatic consists of eights fonts: chromatic, outline, solid, shopworn, inset, stars, stars top, and stars bottom. It is thus more versatile than Page's original design.

Detail of Eight Line, Ten Line, and Twelve Line Chromatic American from *Specimens of Chromatic Wood Type, Borders, &c. Manufactured by Wm. H. Page & Co.* (Greeneville, Connecticut, 1874)

HWT American Chromatic | Chromatic American (William Page, 1874) – Richard Kegler and Terry Wudenbachs (Hamilton Wood Type, 2012)

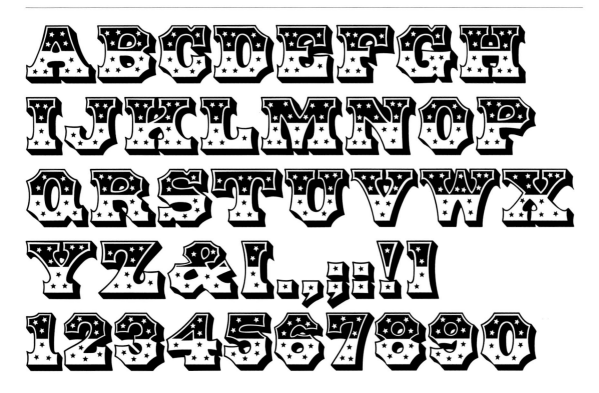

Chromatic | Outline | Solid | Shopworn

Inset | Stars | Stars top | Stars bottom

Gothic

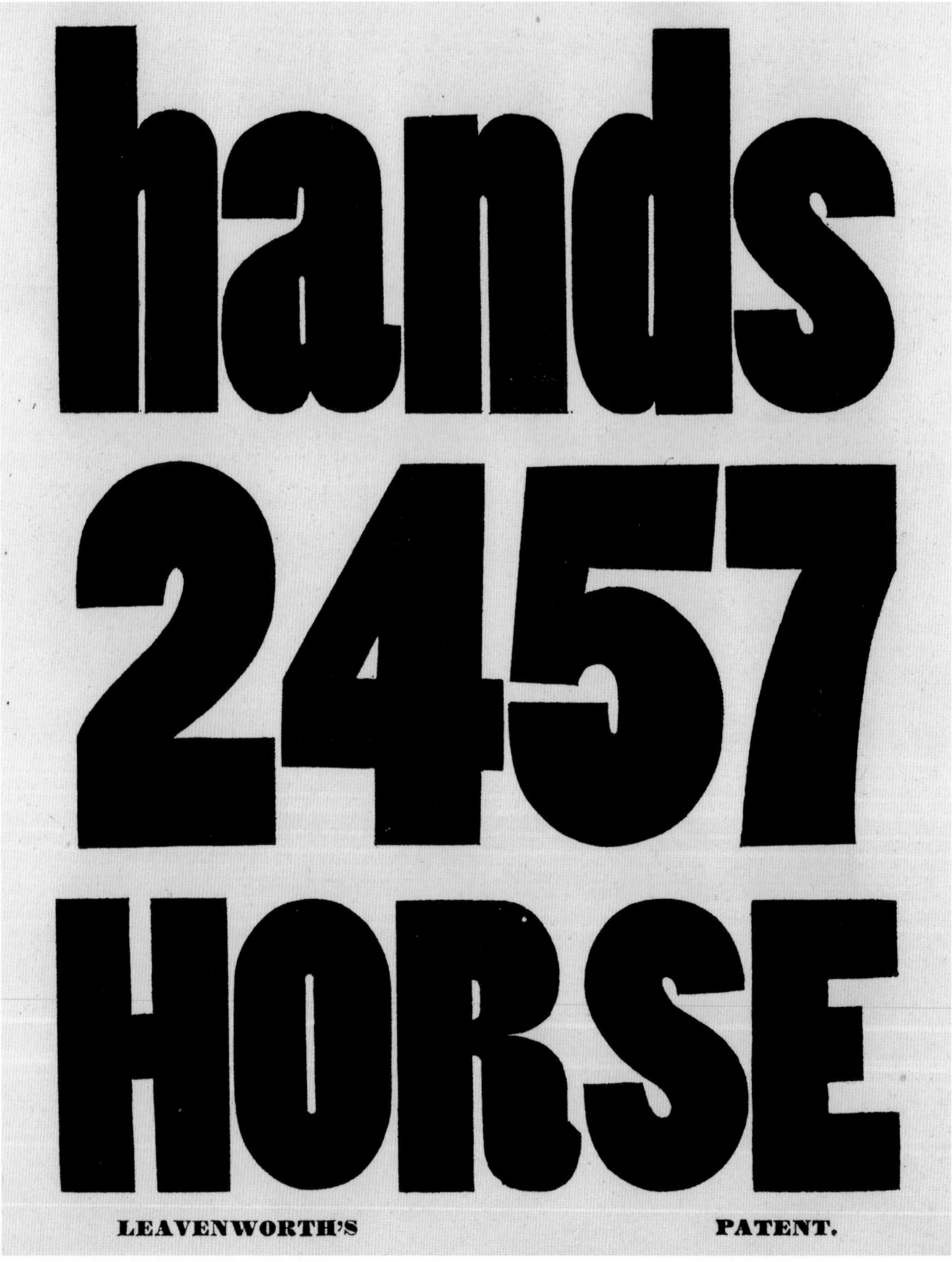

hands
2457
HORSE

LEAVENWORTH'S　　　　　PATENT.

Poplar | Gothic Condensed (J. M. Debow, 1838) – Barbara Lind (Adobe, 1990)

ABCDEFGHIJKLMNOPQ RSTUVWXYZ&abcdefgh ijklmnopqrstuvwxyz fifl 1234567890{[(.,;:!?*)]

William Leavenworth revolutionized the manufacture of wood type when he combined the router with the pantograph in 1834. His Gothic Condensed, first shown in 16- and 12-line sizes in the c. 1838 *Specimen of Leavenworth's Patent Wood Type, Manufactured by J. M. Debow, Allentown, N. J.*, is notable among gothic wood types for having a lowercase. It is the source for Poplar by Barbara Lind. Leavenworth's Gothic Condensed was not shown as a full alphabet in *American Wood Type 1828–1900* (p. 104), but a font is in the Robinson-Pforzheimer Collection now at SUNY Purchase. Poplar is part of the Adobe Wood Type 2 set with Birch, Blackoak (pp. 138–139), Madrone (pp. 136–137), and Willow.

OPPOSITE: 16- and 12-line Gothic Condensed from *Specimen of Leavenworth's Patent Wood Type, Manufactured by J. M. Debow, Allentown, N. J.* (Allentown, New Jersey, c. 1838). Cropped.
COMPARISON (ABOVE): **R**, **a**, **5** from Gothic Condensed vs. Poplar.

FIVE-LINE PICA ORNAMENTED, NO. 6. 5 A
15 lb. 8 oz.

STEAM

FIVE-LINE PICA ORNAMENTED, NO. 7. 5 a and 5 A
17 lb.

COLUMBIANS!

Americans 32

SIX-LINE PICA SHADED, NO. 1. 5 A
29 lb. 8 oz.

CONE

SIX-LINE PICA SHADED, NO. 2. 5 A
18 lb.

BASTILE

SIX-LINE PICA SHADED, NO. 3. 5 a and 5 A
23 lb. 8 oz.

Fine Costume

SIX-LINE PICA ORNAMENTED, NO. 1. 5 A
25 lb. 12 oz.

BIRDS

SIX-LINE PICA ORNAMENTED, NO. 5.

THE

SIX-LINE PICA PERSPECTIVE.

MOAM

SEVEN-LINE PICA SHADED, NO. 2.

TIMES

SEVEN-LINE PICA ORNAMENTED.

HIS

EIGHT-LINE PICA ORNAMENTED, NO. 2.

BIB

EIGHT-LINE PICA ORNAMENTED, NO. 3.

LID

Late Victorian Types

The types in this chapter cover three overlapping but distinct movements in printing and art during the last three decades of the 19th century. The first of them, the Artistic Printing era, began with the publication in 1870 of *Harpel's Typograph, or Book of Specimens* by Oscar H. Harpel (1828–1881), the bulk of which was given over to displays of "artistic" jobbing printing that "harmoniously" mixed as many as seven typefaces, set type on a diagonal or curve, employed complex borders made of mitred brass rule, and used multiple colors to create patterned grounds. For the next two decades all of these strategies (and more) became part of the stock-in-trade of printers desiring to be artistic as a response to competition from lithography houses. The Artistic Printing trend was aided by the steady production of new "fancy" types—sporting delicate filigree, multi-line shading and other complex decoration—that were made possible by engraving designs into soft type metal rather than cutting punches on a shank of steel.

Art Nouveau emerged in France at the beginning of the 1890s and quickly spread throughout Europe and to America. It encompassed all of the design arts, stressing their unity and that of their various constituent parts. This emphasis on *Gesamtkunstwerk* meant that lettering was a central element in graphic design. Like the imagery of the period, it was characterized by an emphasis on organic curves. Capitalizing on this movement European foundries hired artists to design typefaces in the new style, the first of them being Eckmannschrift (1900) by Otto Eckmann (1865–1902) and Auriol (1901) by George Auriol (1863–1938).

Artistic Printing and Art Nouveau typefaces were deliberately ahistorical. Not so those of the Arts and Crafts movement which, under the influence of William Morris (1834–1896) and his Kelmscott Press, looked to the robust printing of the incunabula period for inspiration. Morris modeled his first typeface (the Golden Type) on the type of Nicolas Jenson (see pp. 42–45). Other private press printers followed suit (with the notable exception of the Ashendene Press which, emulated the gotico-antiqua of Sweynheym and Pannartz). These sturdy types were seen as a return to typographic sanity—an antidote not only to the fancy jobbing types of the Victorian period but to the anemic neoclassical typefaces that then dominated text printing.

OPPOSITE: Types from *An Abridged Specimen of Printing Types Made at Bruce's New-York Type-Foundry* (New York: George Bruce's Son & Co., 1869), p. 86 (cropped).

BOSTON TYPE FOUNDRY

EPITAPH  SERIES.

434. Canon Epitaph, 3 A, $6.00.

ORDS OF SORF

437. Double Pica Epitaph, 7 A, $3.25.

STAND 70 & 76 GRAVES
◄EPITAPHS COMPOSED►

448. Pica Epitaph, 14 A, $2.25.

HERE RESTS HIS HEAD UPON THE LAP OF EARTH
A YOUTH, TO FORTUNE AND TO FAME UNKNOWN,

450. Great Primer Epitaph, 9 A, $2.50.

OUNG MAIDS OF 25 & 52 PRIM OLD D
◄COMING AND GOING, PASSING AND GONE►

439. Double Great Primer Epitaph, 5 A, $4.25.

RATIONS AND ORNAME

Epitaph | (Boston Type Foundry, 1885) – Tobias Frere-Jones (Font Bureau, 1993)

AABBCⓒDDEEFFFGGHHIIJJKKLLMM NNOⓞPPQQ2RRSSTTⓉUUVVWWXXYY ZⓩZ&ₐₙₐ12345678890{[(.,;:!?*)]}◇◇◇

John Kimball Rogers (d. 1888) of the Boston Type Foundry established a branch in St. Louis in 1874. Named the Central Type Foundry it was run by James A. St. John (d. 1901), his rival as "agent" for the Boston foundry and the foundry's superintendent Carl Schraubstädter (d. 1896). Upon the death of Rogers, the two men purchased the Boston Type Foundry and thus typefaces appear in the specimen books of both foundries. The Central Foundry became the acknowledged leader of type fashions. *The Inland Printer* (December, 1906) wrote, "Nothing so original was ever seen as the designs of the foundry, which, combining art with oddity, revolutionized the taste of printers everywhere."

Perhaps the Epitaph Series, shown first in the 1885 specimen book of the Boston Type Foundry and subsequently in the 1890 specimen book of the Central Type Foundry, was one of these original designs that combined art with oddity. Certainly it is representative of the wild experimentation that American type foundries engaged in during the 1880s and 1890s as they supplied types to printers seeking to compete with lithographers. Epitaph is a gothic with proto-Art Nouveau features and serifs on a few letters. It was also cast in an Open version.

Tobias Frere-Jones revived Epitaph in the early 1990s at a moment in the digital type era when young designers were experimenting with typefaces that were partially seriffed. This was his way of letting them know that, in the world of type, there was nothing new under the sun, even though technology had changed. Although the original Epitaph had several alternates, Frere-Jones created new ones for all of the remaining letters of the alphabet (save **I**) and for the figure **8**. He also revived the curved logotype **AND** and three geometric ornaments. Epitaph has no lowercase.

OPPOSITE: Epitaph Series from *Specimens from the Boston Type Foundry, John K. Rogers, Agent...* (Boston, 1885).
COMPARISON (ABOVE RIGHT): **A, E** from Epitaph Series vs. Epitaph (Font Bureau).

MOSER

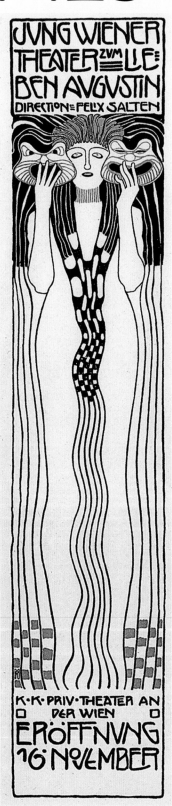

The Vienna Secession was formed in 1897 by a group of artists who, in protest against the traditional art of the day, had resigned from the Kunstlerhaus Genessenschaft (a private artists exhibiting society) and the Akademie de bildende Kunste (Academy of Fine Arts) in Austria. They aspired instead to a renaissance of the arts and crafts that would involve more abstract and purer forms and an emphasis on *Gesamtwerk* (a cross-pollination of all disciplines to form a total work of art).

The Vienna Secession artists are as famous for their graphic design as for their formal artwork. Their posters, postcards, bookplates, and other printed ephemera are characterized by a fecundity of innovative lettering influenced by the theories of Rudolf von Larisch (1856–1934), who stressed balancing figure/ground relationships and matching lettering styles to materials and techniques (see p. 12).

In the period prior to the founding of the Wiener Werkstätte in 1903, the lettering of the Secessionist artists is curvilinear and tightly massed, with letters shaped to fit closely with their neighbors. Paul Shaw based Kolo on thin sans serif lettering by Gustav Klimt (1862–1918), Joseph Maria Olbrich (1867–1908), Josef Auchenthaller (1865–1949) and, especially, Koloman Moser (1868–1918). The original PostScript design (digitized by Garrett Boge) was issued as a set of four fonts (Regular, Narrow, Wide and Alternates). In Kolo OT (digitized by C. J. Dunn) the Alternates have been folded into the Regular design and a large number of ligatures, nested letters, and small hanging letters have been added. There is no lowercase for any of the Kolo variants.

Poster by Koloman Moser for the Jung Wiener Theater (1901).

Kolo Pro | Koloman Moser, Josef Olbrich et al (1890s) – Paul Shaw and C. J. Dunn (LetterPerfect, 1996, 2015)

AABBCCCCDDEEEFGGGGHHHhIJJKK
LLLLLLMMMMNNNNOPPQrRRRSSST
UVVVWWWXXYYYZ&COEREXIJLALBLC
LDLELFLIKLLMOLPLSLTLULVLYMMNDNFNK
NNOOQURATCHTHTTTYZZOO
ABCDEEFGHIJKLMNOPQRSTUVWXYYZ
1234567890{[(.,;:!?*)]}

ABCDEEFGHIJKLMNOPQRSTUVWXYYZ

THEATER

THEATER

COMPARISON: Word from the Jung Wiener Theater poster vs. word set in Kolo OT Pro with ligatures **TH**, **EA** and **ER**.

MACKINTOSH

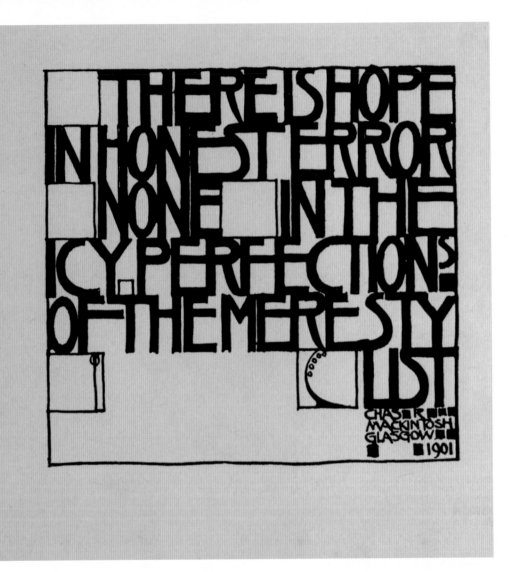

"There is hope in honest error...." Quotation designed by Charles Rennie Mackintosh (1901).

ITC Rennie Mackintosh Bold and Ornaments | Charles Rennie Mackintosh (1890s) – Phill Grimshaw (ITC, 1996)

AAABBCCDDEEFFGGHHIJKKLL̈MMNNºOPPPQ℘
RRRRSSSSTUUVWẄXXYYZZ℧&ATEAFIFLITIALELL
∞∞◊◊SSTHTT TTᴬᴰFOR℘ᴼᴼᴶTHE1234567890{[(.,:;!?*)]}

𝔸𝔹𝔻𝔼𝔽𝔾ℍ𝕀𝕁𝕂𝕃𝕄ℕ𝕆𝕡ℚℝ𝕊𝕋𝕌𝕍𝕎𝕏𝕐ℤℭ

The Scottish architect Charles Rennie Mackintosh (1868–1928) was the leading figure in the Glasgow School, a small Art Nouveau movement in fin-de-siècle Scotland. In 1897 he created a poster for Miss Cranston's Buchanan Street tearooms. It was the first of a fruitful series of increasingly ambitious commissions for its owner Kate Cranston (1849–1934) that culminated in the renowned Willow Tearooms. With the Willow Tearooms, completed in 1903 for her Sauchiehall Street address, Mackintosh was responsible for everything: the interior design and furniture, exterior architectural treatment, and the full detail of the internal layout, including the tableware. It was a total work of art.

Mackintosh's 1897 poster for the Buchanan Street tearooms is marked by spare but stylized sans serif lettering banded within a box and arranged asymmetrically that contrasted with the fluid, curvilinear lettering of Art Nouveau elsewhere. This distinctive lettering, best exemplified by Mackintosh's 1901 rendering of a quotation by J. D. Sedding (1838–91), provided the basis for ITC Rennie Mackintosh. The typeface, designed by Phill Grimshaw (1950–98), was intended to accompany a major Mackintosh retrospective at the Victoria & Albert Museum in 1996.

ITC Rennie Mackintosh is a titling face with numerous alternate characters, ligatures, logotypes, cameo initials, and ornaments. Many of the alternate characters, especially the more decorative ones, have been invented by Grimshaw with features derived from Mackintosh's celebrated furniture designs. Another interpretation of Mackintosh's lettering is Willow (1990) by Tony Forster (1941–2008), Grimshaw's mentor.

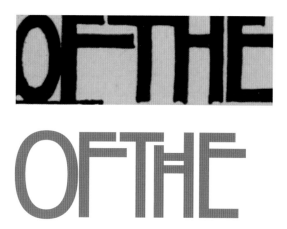

COMPARISON: Words from the Mackintosh design on the opposite page vs. logotypes **OF** and **THE** from ITC Rennie Mackintosh.

Golden Type

[Image of letterpress text detail showing fragments of words: "nly he ascended lightl", "nt with a grete paas a", "he passed so grete a sp", "grete philosopher, reh", "lanete, hath the thykn", "may goo in a playne w"]

William Morris was a prolific designer of interiors, furniture, stained glass, wallpaper, tapestries, carpets, tiles, books and typefaces. He was also a calligrapher, poet, novelist, essayist, translator of Norse sagas, and socialist. The Kelmscott Press, the venture he established in 1891, inspired the private press movement of the Arts and Crafts period. Morris designed the typefaces for his books with the punches being cut by Edward Prince (1846–1923). The first of his three types was the Golden Type, first used in *The Story of the Glittering Plain* (1891) but named after *The Golden Legend* (1892), which had been intended as the Press' first title. Morris' other two typefaces, named Troy (1892) and Chaucer (1893), were rotundas.

Morris based his Golden Type on the roman of Nicolas Jenson (see pp. 42–45). "This type," he wrote, "I studied with much care, getting it photographed to a big scale, and drawing it over many times before I began designing my own letter; so that though I think I mastered the essence of it, I did not copy it servilely; in fact, my Roman type, especially in the lower case, tends rather more to the Gothic than does Jenson's."

ITC Golden Type by Helga Jörgenson (b. 1955) and Sigrid Engelmann (b. 1953) is a fairly direct copy of Morris' design with little added other than a few punctuation marks. The typeface looks very different printed offset than it does in the books issued by the Kelmscott Press where letterpress provides a third dimension of depth. P22 has also issued a revival of the Golden Type as part of a Morris Set (2002) with an interpretation of the Troy Type, both designed by Richard Kegler.

Detail from *The Golden Legend* by Jacobus de Voragine (Hammersmith [London]: The Kelmscott Press, 1892), p. 67.

ITC Golden Type | William Morris and Edward Prince (1891) – Helga Jörgenson and Sigrid Engelmann (ITC, 1989)

ABCDEFGHIJKLMNOPQRSTUV
WXYZ&abcdefghijklmnopqrstuvwx
yz&abcdefghijklmnopqqrstuvwxyzfifl
1234567890123456789O{[(.,;:!?*)]}☾

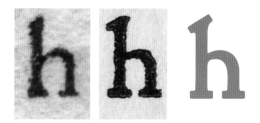

COMPARISON: **M, h** from roman by Nicolas Jenson | Golden Type by William Morris | ITC Golden Type.

Doves Roman

ng : the great revival in pr

under our own eyes, is the

re he was a Printer was a Ca

r, WILLIAM MORRIS

he whole duty of Typogra

communicate to the ima

e way, the thought or ima

icated by the Author. A

tiful typography is not to s

interest of the thing thou

eyed by the symbol, a be

Detail from *The Ideal Book or Book Beautiful: A Tract on Calligraphy, Printing and Illustration & On the Book Beautiful as a Whole* by Thomas James Cobden-Sanderson (Hammersmith [London]: The Doves Press, 1900), p. 6.

Doves Type | Percy Tiffin and Edward Prince (Doves Press, 1900) – Robert Green (Typespec, 2015)

ABCDEFGHIJKLMNOPQQRSTUVW
XYZ&ABCDEFGHIJKLMNOPQQRSTUVWXYZ
abcdefghijklmnopqrstuvwxyzQUQuRANº
&fbfffhfifkflffbffhffiiffkffl ry ty
12345678901234567890{[(.,;:!¿*)]}℃

The Doves Press was established in 1900 with Emery Walker (1851–1933) and Thomas James Cobden-Sanderson (1840–1922), two of William Morris' associates, as partners. Like Morris, they turned to Jenson as a model for their proprietary typeface. However, the Doves Press roman, cut by Edward Prince based on drawings by Percy Tiffin (and with Walker overseeing things), was "freed from the accidental irregularities due to imperfect cutting and casting and the serifs altered in some cases." Lighter and more regular than the Golden Type, it was created only in 16 pt.

The partnership between the two men soon began to sour as each had differing priorities, with Walker engaged in a photo-engraving business among other endeavors and Cobden-Sanderson more invested in the private press. The partnership was dissolved in 1909 amid increased acrimony, with an agreement leaving Cobden-Sanderson to print with the type until his death, whereupon it would pass to the younger Walker.

However, unwilling to countenance the possibility of anyone else, including Walker, using the Doves Press roman, Cobden-Sanderson began plotting to get rid of it. In 1913 he dumped the punches and matrices into the Thames. Then, from August 1916 until early 1917, he regularly and ritually dumped the cast type into the river as well.

In 2014 Robert Green (b. 1965), as part of his attempt to design a digital version of the Doves Press roman, searched the Thames and found some of the types. A subsequent dive by the Port Authority recovered 150 pieces. However, the Doves Type, a faithful revival of the Doves Press roman, is based on printed sources not on the corroded metal types. In making his typeface Green eschewed any improvements, resorting only to the inevitable additions needed for modern communication (e.g., accented characters, the @ sign, broader punctuation, etc.).

COMPARISON: **M**, **h** from Doves Press roman vs. Doves Type.

YZUHARL
PSVDLTG!
TBXNCJQ

Z.

Mte Palatino
8.044
1950

Roma '50

Z. Nov. 1950
>AURELIA<
Serifen a-d

d-Serifen ok

Ziffern
L3
Versalhöhe ?

A O und U gleich breit
Punkte
und E
zum ansehen

Die Konturen der
Buchstaben für
die AURELIA
etwa wie bei der
COCHIN-Antiqua

20th Century Seriffed Types

In 1885 Linn Boyd Benton (1844–1932) invented a device variously called the Benton punchcutting machine or Benton engraving machine that sped up the production of type. It did not cut punches but instead engraved matrices from pattern plates via a pantograph that were then used to cast type. The patterns were made from drawings, which meant that the design of type no longer required punchcutting skill. This opened the profession to anyone with letter-drawing skills.

The profession of type designer emerged out of the Arts and Crafts movement of the 1890s. Although a small number were employed by type foundries and composing machine companies as staff artists or art directors, the majority were freelance designers or letterers who created typefaces as a sideline. Rare was the individual like Frederic W. Goudy, who was able to sustain a career as an independent type designer.

In the first half of the 20th century—the dusk of the metal type era—many of these designers were inspired by the ideas and ideals of the Arts and Crafts movement. Following William Morris they often focused on making designs, however new, that were in the oldstyle vein. This was especially true of Goudy. Some of them, trained as calligraphers following the revival of calligraphy by Edward Johnston (1872–1944) and influenced by the notion—expounded by Thomas James Cobden-Sanderson (see p. 167)—that calligraphy was the basis of typography, began their designs with broad-edged pen sketches instead of outline drawings of letters. The prime example of this approach is the oeuvre of Hermann Zapf. In contrast, other designers—especially those working as commercial artists like Oswald Cooper (1879–1940)—were hired to create typefaces intended to take advantage of trends in art and design or simply to fill gaps in a foundry's catalogue. Advertising and publicity were the driving forces behind such designs more than aesthetic ideals.

Twentieth-century seriffed typefaces often have features inspired by multiple sources filtered through personal aesthetics. Consequently, they do not fit easily into standard historical categories.

OPPOSITE: Undated proof of Aurelia (the original name of Sistina), rubbings from Rome made by Hermann Zapf in October 1950, and drawings for Aurelia (dated November 1950).

Palatino

ABCDEFGHIJKLMN

OPQYZRSTUVWX

ÄÖÜQuÆŒÇØ IHK

123456890 $ 123456890

abcdefghijklmnopqrs

tuvwxyzäöüæœçchck

tzßfffif1ft Typographie,

im Grunde zweidimen=

sionale Architektur, ver

¶&.·-=.,:.!?'.,"»«/*§□◇†[(H)]

åøáâàéêèëíîìïíóôòòúûùùžš

TuWuVu

48' Palatino / D.Stempel AG, 10. 12. 51

Palatino Nova | Palatino (Hermann Zapf, Stempel, 1948) – Harmann Zapf and Akira Kobayashi (Linotype, 2005)

ABCDEFGHIJKLMNOPQRSTUVW
XYZ&&ABCDEFGHIJKLMNOPQRSTUVW
xyz&abcdefghijklmnopqrstuvwyz
ctetfffhfifjflftſpſtththttz ffiffjfflfft
12345678901234567890{[(.,;:!?*)]}¶

Palatino, first cast by the Stempel foundry in 1949, established the reputation of Hermann Zapf as a type designer. As type technology has changed over the succeeding decades, Zapf continually redesigned the face with the last version being Palatino Nova, made with the aid of Akira Kobayashi. These redesigns—eighteen variations involving at least twenty-eight different sets of master patterns between 1949 and 1953 alone—are recounted in minute detail in *Palatino: The Natural History of a Typeface* (2016) by Robert Bringhurst.

Zapf carried them out both to correct features that had been designed for the limitations of specific technologies (such as short descenders to accommodate the German common line), but also to reflect his changing sense of what Palatino should ideally look like. Compared to its foundry forebear, Palatino Nova has shorter ascenders, longer descenders, fewer calligraphic features (e.g. **X**, **x** and **y**), serifs on the midstrokes of **E** and **F**, a longer tail on **Q**, steeper spines on **S** and **s**, a shorter **t**, and other smaller adjustments. It is a design that is radically different and yet the same.

Since its introduction into the United States in the early 1950s, as both foundry type and Linotype matrices, Palatino has been a popular book face. However, Zapf intended it to be an advertising type. For book typography he subsequently designed Aldus (1954), a narrower version of Palatino with a smaller x-height, sharper features and fewer calligraphic elements. Aldus was redesigned by Zapf and Kobayashi as Aldus Nova and incorporated into the new Palatino Nova family.

hpy hpy

OPPOSITE: 48 pt (Didot) Palatino proof from D. Stempel AG (dated 12 October 1951).
COMPARISON (ABOVE): **h**, **p**, **y** from 1951 Palatino proof vs. Palatino Nova.

MICHELANGELO
SISTINA

ABC
DEFGHI
JKLMNOP
QRSTUV
WXYZ
KQRS

ABC
DEFGHI
JKLMNOP
QRSTUV
WXZ
& Q

In the fall of 1950 Hermann Zapf made an eventful visit to Italy. The trip resulted in the design of three of his most famous typefaces: Michelangelo (1950), Sistina (1951), and Optima (see pp. 30–31 and 230–231). The first two were titling faces inspired by inscriptional lettering Zapf saw in Rome. Despite their names, both were promoted by Stempel as companions to Palatino. When Zapf, with the assistance of Akira Kobayashi, redesigned Palatino as Palatino Nova, he also revamped Michelangelo and Sistina and subsumed them into the new family as Palatino Nova Titling and Palatino Nova Imperial respectively.

Several letters in Palatino Nova Titling are significantly changed from Michelangelo: **G** has been reshaped,

the hook of **J** eliminated, the tail of **Q** both straightened and lengthened, the spine of **S** sloped more, the opening between the arms of **Y** reduced, the top of **3** curved, and the bowl of **9** reduced. Fewer changes have been made to Sistina. The alternate narrow **L** and **T** are gone, but an alternate **U** without a leg (an original design that was never released) and **W** with uncrossed strokes have been added. The terminal of **J** and the tails of the two **Q**s are different. Despite the overhaul, both Palatino Nova Titling and Palatino Nova Imperial retain the distinctive character of their forebears.

24 pt Michelangelo (left) and 24 pt Sistina (right) printed on Johannot paper by Michael Babcock, Interrobang Letterpress (2013). The Sistina **Y** is missing.

Palatino Nova Titling | Michelangelo (Hermann Zapf, Stempel, 1950) – Hermann Zapf and Akira Kobayashi (Linotype, 2005)

ABCDEFGHIJKLMNOPQRSTUV WXYZ&1234567890{[(.,;:!?*)]}·¶

Palatino Nova Imperial | Sistina (Hermann Zapf, Stempel, 1951) – Hermann Zapf and Akira Kobayashi (Linotype, 2005)

ABCDEFGHIJKLMNOPQQRRSTT UUVWWXYZABCDEFGHIJKLMNPQ RRSTTUVWXYZ&&1234567890 {[(.,;:!?*)]}¶

COMPARISON (TOP): **G**, **Q** from Michelangelo vs. Palatino Nova Titling.
COMPARISON (BOTTOM): **Q**s from Sistina vs. Palatino Nova Imperial.

Cartier

Carl Dair (1912–1967), was Canada's first internation- ally recognized graphic designer. In 1956 he received a government fellowship to study type making at the Joh. Enschedé en Zonen type foundry in Haarlem under letter engraver P. H. Radisch. Ten years later Dair achieved his goal of creating a uniquely Canadian type- face, Cartier Roman and Italic. Mono Lino Typesetting in Toronto released it as a film type in 1967, Canada's Centennial Year. Dair designed the roman with heavy baseline serifs to aid readability; and designed the italic—under the influence of Francesco Griffo—without separate capitals. Dair's decisions were criticized at the time and at his death, later that year, Cartier was consid- ered to be unfinished despite its release.

In 2000, Canadian lettering artist and type designer Rod McDonald (b. 1946) revived Cartier as Cartier Book. The new typeface, especially in the italic, is a root and branch rethinking of Dair's design rather than a blind homage. McDonald's goal was to make Cartier a func- tional text face rather than a historical curiosity, while retaining enough of the original character of Dair's design to justify the name Cartier Book. He radically altered several of the features that were distinctive about Cartier, most notably the form of the serifs in the roman and the entire structure of the italic.

The original Cartier Italic, inspired by Renaissance chancery italics, was nearly upright and very narrow with *corsiva formata* endings to ascenders and closed descenders for **g** and **y**. McDonald widened the letters, added serifs to the ascenders, flattened the exit strokes, and opened up the **g** and **y**. He also added a set of cap- itals. The result is an italic that is in harmony with the roman as modern type users expect.

Detail of paste-up (16 January 1967) of Cartier Roman and Italic by Carl Dair with markings for unit values of each letter.

Cartier Book Pro | Carl Dair (Mono Lino, 1967) – Rod McDonald (Monotype, 2000)

ABCDEFGHIJKLMNOPQRSTUVWXYZ&
abcdefghijklmnopqrstuvwxyz&
abcdefghijklmnopqrstuvwxyz ff fi fj fl ffi ffl
1234567890{[(.,;:!*)]}¶

Cartier Book Pro Italic | Carl Dair (Mono Lino, 1967) – Rod McDonald (Monotype, 2000)

ABCDEFGHIJKLMNOPQRSTUVWXYZ&
abcdefghijklmnopqrstuvwxyz&
abcdefghijklmnopqrstuvwxyz ff fi fj fl ffi ffl
1234567890{[(.,;:!*)]}¶

a a a

h h

COMPARISON (TOP): original drawing of **a** by Dair, Cartier Roman **a** and Cartier Book.
COMPARISON (BOTTOM): Cartier Italic **h** vs. Cartier Book Italic.

Goudy Oldstyle

HE type family idea is a creation of the American Type Founders Company. It is easily the greatest economy ever effected in display composition and it saves greatly in the cost of composition because the compositor can quickly visualize his work. It also preserves automatically the typographic harmony of display composition. What position would the Printing Industry be in today without the many famous type families introduced by the American Type Founders Company; would not your own typography be barren

Goudy Oldstyle (ATF, 1916) is the best known of the more than 100 typefaces—the exact number has been open to dispute—designed by Frederic W. Goudy. From the moment it was released it was a huge hit with printers, becoming an advertising staple until World War II, and continuing after that to remain popular even as Goudy's reputation waned. Despite its success, Goudy was not happy with the design of Goudy Oldstyle. ATF had truncated the descenders to make them fit their American Common Line, thus diminishing the typeface's air of elegance. Goudy refused to do any more

work with the foundry beyond two designs already in progress, and so the Goudy Oldstyle family was built out by Morris Fuller Benton.

With LTC Goudy Oldstyle, Lanston Type Company has brought back Goudy's original long descenders while providing the short ones as alternates. The character set also includes small capitals, oldstyle figures, quaint ligatures and an Aldus leaf. All of these features make it more suitable for book use than the original ATF version.

Detail from *A Composite Showing of Goudy Types* (Jersey City, New Jersey: American Type Founders, 1927).

LTC Goudy Oldstyle Pro | Goudy Oldstyle (Frederic W. Goudy, American Type Founders, 1916) – (Lanston Type Company, 2005)

ABCDEFGHIJKLMNOPQRSTUV
WXYZ&ABCDEFGHIJKLMNOPQRSTUV
wxyz&abcdefgghijjklmnoppqqrsſtuv
wxyyzctfbffffhfifjfjfkflffbffhffiiffjffjffkfflst
ffı2345678901234567890{[(.,;:!?*)]}¶℘

COMPARISON (TOP): **E, g** from ATF Goudy Oldstyle and LTC Goudy Oldstyle Pro.
COMPARISON (BOTTOM): Distinctive letters in ATF Goudy Oldstyle.

Burgess

Lanston Monotype pattern letters stamped No. 54 [Starling Burgess] and Series 362 [Times New Roman], c. 1904.

Starling | Times New Roman (Stanley Morison and Victor Lardent, Monotype Corporation, 1932) or Number 54 (William Starling Burgess, c. 1904) – Mike Parker (Font Bureau, 2009)

ABCDEFGHIJKLMNOPQRSTUV
WXYZ&ABCDEFGHIJKLMNOPQRSTUV
WXYZ&abcdefghijklmnopqrstuvwxyz
ff fi fj ffi ffl 11234567890I234567890
{[(.,;:!?*)]}¶

Burgess by Mike Parker (1929–2014) is as much a polemic as it is a typeface. Parker, Director of Typographic Development at Mergenthaler Linotype from 1961 to 1981, co-founder of Bitstream and typographic advisor to Font Bureau, wrote an article in 1994 arguing that Times New Roman was not the work of Stanley Morison and Victor Lardent (1905–1968) as widely believed, but instead that of an American yacht designer named William Starling Burgess (1878–1947). His thesis was that c. 1904 Burgess had designed a typeface for his own use, ostensibly assisted by the draughtsman E. Shand, which was manufactured by the Lanston Monotype Company but never paid for. The roman design (labeled No. 54 by Lanston) was subsequently offered by Lanston for potential sale to Time magazine in 1921/1922 during its start-up phase, but never adopted. At that point, Parker theorizes, the design was transferred to the Monotype Corporation in England where, in 1930, Morison, strug-

gling with the development of a new typeface for The Times of London newspaper, stumbled across it and appropriated it wholesale.

It is a controversial theory, full of intrigue and supposition, with key documents and supporting material—other than a few pantographic pattern plates—unfortunately lost. A comprehensive rebuttal by Harold Berliner, Nicolas Barker, John Dreyfus and Jim Rimmer was published in 1998. However, sticking to his theory Parker subsequently designed Starling, based on the artifacts he had uncovered and a 1990s PostScript digitization done by Gerard Giampa (1950–2009). The differences between Starling and Times New Roman (called Times Roman in the Linotype version) are minuscule. However, Starling Italic by Parker, based on incomplete trials for an italic by Burgess (labeled No. 55 by Lanston), is radically different from Times Roman Italic.

Gh Gh

COMPARISON: **G, h** from Times New Roman vs. Starling.

Diotima Italic

Diotima-Kursiv

ABCDEFGHIJKLMNOP
QRSTUVWXYZ
abcdefghijklmnopqrstuvwxyz
12345 & 67890

Schopenhauers Aphorismen

GEDICHTE

Philosophie der Neuzeit

SCHRIFTGIESSEREI D. STEMPEL AG FRANKFURT AM MAIN

Diotima Classic LT Pro, Pro Italic | Diotima (Gudrun Zapf-von Hesse, Stempel, 1954) – Gudrun Zapf-von Hesse and Akira Kobayashi (Linotype, 2009)

ABCDEFGHIJKLMNOPQRSTUVWX YZ&ABCDEFGHJKLMNOPQRSTUVWXYZ& abcdefghijklmnopqrstuvwxyzfffifl ft ffiffl1234567890{[(.,;:!?*)]}

Gudrun Zapf-von Hesse (b. 1918) is a calligrapher and type designer, one of the few women in the profession prior to the digital era. She was married to Hermann Zapf. Her typefaces, like those of her husband, reflect the influence of the broad-edged pen without being calligraphic scripts. Diotima (1954), her first typeface and widely viewed as her masterwork, is more of a transitional design than an oldstyle like Palatino. It is characterized by a surprisingly wide roman supplemented by a narrow and elegant italic.

With the assistance of Akira Kobayashi, Zapf-von Hesse redesigned Diotima as Diotima Classic to fit the requirements of digital design and offset printing.

In the roman the ascenders have been slightly shortened and the descenders lengthened; the short J has become a long J, the tail of Q has been reshaped, the tail of y has been seriffed, and the 2 has been radically redrawn. The italic has been made wider; A has lost its head serif, the counter of B has been closed, and the f has been given more curve, while the x has been entirely redrawn. The beautiful Ariadne swash capitals (1954) designed by Zapf-von Hesse as an accompaniment to Diotima have not been revived.

OPPOSITE: Diotima Italic specimen from D. Stempel AG (c.1952).
COMPARISON (ABOVE): **x, y** from Diotima Italic vs. Diotima Classic LT Pro.

Cooper

Lettering artist and type designer Oswald Cooper is best known for his eponymous Cooper Black, a typeface that polarizes designers. Cooper Fullface, his attempt at designing a more friendly neoclassical typeface, was released by Barnhart Brothers & Spindler in 1929 (but renamed Cooper Modern by ATF after it took over production, following the closing of BB&S that same year). Most strokes, including the hairline serifs, are slightly bowed and the curved letters are very loosely drawn. Nothing is mechanical or rigid. Cooper said of Cooper Fullface that it "differs from Bodoni in that its serifs are rounded, and its main stems drawn freely, with a sug-

gestion of curve in almost every line." Like most foundry types, the **f** and **j** were designed to avoid kerning.

Cooper Fullface never reached the same level of success as Cooper Black and was virtually forgotten by the 1990s when Dave Farey (b. 1943) revived it as ITC Ozwald. His design accentuates the curviness of Cooper's letters, especially adding more swagger to the stems and widening the letters even more. The image of Cooper Fullface shown above is a paste-up of characters (sadly falling apart) showing the design in progress. Note the two forms of **s** and the rejected forms of **e** and **f**.

Paste-up of pen-and-ink trial letters for Cooper Fullface (c. 1928).

ITC Ozwald | Cooper Fullface (Oswald Cooper, Barnhart Brothers & Spindler, 1927) – Dave Farey (ITC, 1992)

**ABCDEFGHIJK
LMNOPQRSTUV
WXYZ&abcdefg
hijklmnopqrstu
vwxyz12345678
90{[((-.,;::?)]}⟨**

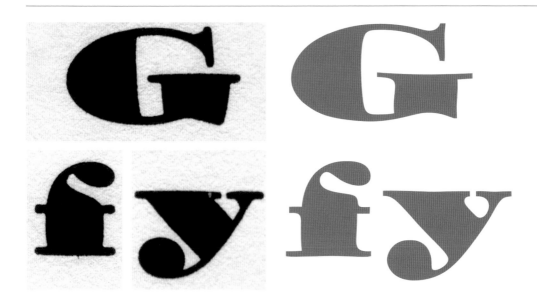

COMPARISON: **G**, **f**, **y** from Cooper Fullface (Cooper Modern) vs. ITC Ozwald.

Joanna

ing a new form; he is only concerned to make well
or ill the form with which he is familiar.

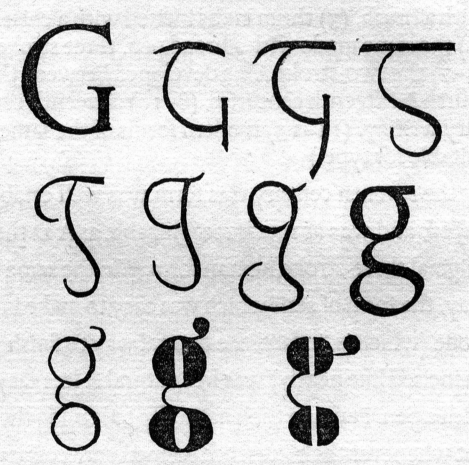

(Figure 3 (1–8) shows the evolution of the lowercase g from the Roman original. 9–11 are comic
modern varieties having more relation to pairs of
spectacles than to lettering—as though the designer
had said: A pair of spectacles is rather like a g; I will
make a g rather like a pair of spectacles.)

Joanna Nova | Joanna (Eric Gill, Monotype, 1931) – Ben Jones (Monotype, 2015)

ABCDEFGHIJKLMNOPQRSTUVW
XYZ&ABCDEFGHIJKLMNOPQRSTUVW
xyzabcdefghijklmnopqrstuvwxyzfb
ff fh fi fj fk fl ffb ffh ffi ffj ffk ffl 1234567
8901234567890{[(.,;:!?*)]}¶

Eric Gill (1882–1940) is principally known for his Gill Sans typeface, but to many typographers his best typeface is Joanna, named after his daughter Joan. It was designed in 1931 for use in books printed by Hague & Gill, the press Gill had just established with his son-in-law René Hague. One of its first uses—and its most memorable—was to set the original edition of *An Essay on Typography* (1931), Gill's first treatise on aesthetics. The type was initially produced in a small quantity by the Caslon foundry for hand composition. The Monotype Corporation then recut Joanna for the sole use of publisher J. M. Dent, not releasing it publicly until 1958 when Dent's license expired.

Joanna is a light slab serif of condensed proportions with humanist features. Its italic is an even narrower sloped roman, influenced by Stanley Morison's theory, expressed in "Towards an Ideal Italic" (*The Fleuron* no. 5 [1926]), that a sloped roman was a better companion for a roman than a true italic.

In the course of revising Gill Sans in 2015, Monotype decided to also revise Joanna. The task was undertaken by Ben Jones (b. 1980). Unlike Gill Sans Nova, which is characterized by an overabundance of alternates reflecting the convoluted history of the typeface and its extended family, Joanna Nova only has three alternate forms (**1**, **3**, and **5**). Terrance Weinzierl (b. 1984) drew Joanna Sans Nova as a companion face.

OPPOSITE: Detail from *An Essay on Typography* by Eric Gill (London: Sheed & Ward, 1931), p. 32.
COMPARISON (ABOVE): **R**, **g** from Joanna and Joanna Nova.

Méridien

ureuse répartition
ines et de montag
GIONS DE FRAN

Adrian Frutiger was, with Hermann Zapf, one of the two greatest type designers of the 20th century. Although principally celebrated for his design of sans serifs (especially Univers [1957], Frutiger [1976], and Avenir [1989]), he was just as adept at seriffed faces. The first of his typefaces to garner widespread praise was Méridien, a book type with latin (wedge-shaped) serifs, released by Deberny & Peignot in 1957. Although widely used in France, the typeface never gained as much popularity in other countries.

Since the mid-1980s the notion of designing matching serif and sans serif types has become increasingly commonplace. In order to keep up with this trend Linotype—in consultation with Frutiger—decided to revise Méridien, rename it and pair it with the sans serif Frutiger (1974). This was not difficult to do since many of Frutiger's typefaces share a common aesthetic and underlying structure. The major change is that the characters of Frutiger Serif are slightly narrower (most noticeable in the lowercase letters with bowls) than those of Méridien, and the descenders have been lengthened. The narrow **f**, designed to avoid kerning, has been kept intact. Akira Kobayashi assisted Frutiger in the redesign.

Detail from Méridien specimen (Deberny & Peignot, 1957).

Frutiger Serif LT Pro | Méridien (Adrian Frutiger, Deberny & Peignot, 1954) – Adrian Frutiger and Akira Kobayashi (Linotype, 2008)

ABCDEFGHIJKLMNOPQRSTUVWX
YZ&&ABCDEFGHIJKLMNOPQRSTUVW
xyz&&abcdefghijklmnopqrstuvwx
yzfffifl ft ffi ffl1234567890l234567890
{[(.,;:!?*)]}§

Gg Gg

ay3&

COMPARISON: **G, g** from Méridien vs. Frutiger Serif. BELOW: Distinctive characters in Frutiger Serif.

onntag,

24.

märz

1,30 uhr

stad

matinee der

bauhaus

bül

Grotesques and Gothics

¶ Amidst several lines of decorative types in his type specimen of 1816 William Caslon IV included a single line of capitals (WM CASLON JUNR LETTERFOUNDER) labeled Two Lines English Egyptian. Contrary to its name it was not a slab serif, but a sans serif, the first instance of the third major category of jobbing type to emerge in the first decade and a half of the 19th century.

In naming his monolinear type, Caslon IV had followed the practice of the sign-writing trade of his day. It was Vincent Figgins who first employed the term sans serif, displaying a 2-line Great Primer Sans-Serif in his specimen book of 1832. Like Caslon's type it was capitals only, but it differed in that its letter widths were more condensed and less classical. It looked like a slab serif with its serifs removed, which is one theory of how this style of type came to be invented.

Figgins's descriptive name—a rare instance of a type style being denoted by a feature it lacked—was taken up by some founders (though under variant spellings such as sans seriff, sans ceriph, and sans surryph), but others applied names with different frames of reference: antique, doric and even grotesque. While the latter (often shortened to grot in speech) came to be the preferred name in England and in Germany (as grotesk), the French called it antique, and the Americans labeled it gothic after their first sans serif (shown by the Boston Type and Stereotype Foundry in 1832). (The nomenclature of typefaces has been a chaotic mess from the moment that typefounders found themselves compelled to differentiate their types from those of their competitors.)

The first instances of a lowercase sans serif, a 7-line Grotesque (the first use of the term) from William Thorowgood and two sizes of a Gothic Condensed from the Philadelphia foundry of Johnson & Smith, occurs in 1834. However, the idea did not become widespread until the second half of the 19th century. The grotesques were intended for advertising and, as such, there was little need for a lowercase. Made by the wood type manufacturers as well as the type foundries, they joined fat faces and egyptians as the preferred type styles on broadsides and multi-sheet posters, often mixed together but segregated by line. These grotesques were made in a range of widths from triple extra condensed to double expanded to accommodate the competing imperatives to save space and to grab attention.

OPPOSITE: Detail of *Matinee der Bauhausbühne im Stadttheater Breslau* poster by Erich Mende (1929). Set in Schelter Grotesk.

Smaller and lighter grotesques of normal proportions—with a lowercase as a regular feature—appeared in the middle of the 19th century for use in newspaper advertising, circulars, billheads, trade cards, and labels. The trend was led by German and American foundries. Both Johann Christian Bauer (1802–1867) and the Dresler'sche Giesserei (owned by Carl Meyer) issued a Mittel Grotesque in 1858 with a lowercase. The New York foundry of Charles White & Co. showed three small sizes (Pica, Great Primer and Two-Line Pica) of a lighter gothic with a lowercase in their 1860 catalogue, though Sara Soskolne believes it may have been cut as late as 1862.

Although 19th-century typefoundries released grotesques in a huge array of widths and weights, they did so without any coordinated plan. This changed in the first decade of the 20th century. In 1908, American Type Founders in New Jersey

A spread from a Eurostile specimen (Società Nebiolo Torino, c.1962).

advertised the cohort of Franklin Gothic (1902), Alternate Gothic (1903), Monotone Gothic (1907), Lightline Gothic (1908), and News Gothic (1908)—all designed by Morris Fuller Benton with varying weights, widths, and sloped versions called "italics"—as a single family despite their differing names. At the same time, H. Berthold GmbH in Berlin announced that Akzidenz Grotesk (1898) was available as a family. Other founders soon followed suit with Bauer developing Venus—acquired from Flinsch—into a family and Stephenson, Blake & Co. adding more weights and widths to its existing set of numbered grotesques.

Despite these developments, the sans serif remained a jobbing face, shunned from being used in books as uncouth and lowbred until the 1920s. The advocates of the "new typography" (*die neue typographie*) at the Bauhaus and elsewhere in Weimar Germany elevated these pedestrian types to favored status. In the view of the new typographers, the grotesques were free of historical associations, available in large families (unlike seriffed faces), appropriate for the new machine age, and the typographic equivalent of the proletariat (anonymous, hardworking, and invisible).

In the first two decades following the end of World War II, Swiss designers became the vanguard of modernist design. Akzidenz Grotesk was their default typeface (with Monotype Grotesque used at small sizes). But the increased popularity and spread of modernism spurred foundries to design newer, more rationally constructed sans serifs (called neo-grotesques) as alternatives to Akzidenz Grotesk. The turning point was 1957 when Haas released Neue Haas Grotesk (later renamed Helvetica), Bauer put out Folio by Konrad Bauer (1903–1970) and Walter Baum (1921–2007), and Deberny & Peignot issued Univers by Adrian Frutiger in a fully coordinated and carefully calibrated family of twenty-one numbered members. The sans serif had finally arrived as an accepted member of typographic society.

The first sans serif with a lowercase. From *Thorowgood's New Specimens of Printing Types* (London: Fann Street Foundry, 1834).

Gothic no. 4

O! grant, indulgent Heaven, no rising storm may darken, with black wings, this glorious scene!

CLEANLINESS ESSENTIAL TO HEALTH. 123

In each smiling countenance appears fresh blooming health and universal joy.

MODERATION PERSONIFIED. 1865.

Cowed by the ruling rod and haughty frowns of pedagogues severe.

PRETTY SHAPE AND SLENDER.

Detail of Long Primer Gothic No. 4 and Pica Gothic No. 4 from *Specimen Book of Plain and Ornamental Printing Types, Borders, Rules, Cuts, Etc., Made by Farmer, Little & Company* (New York, 1867).

Marr Sans | Farmer & Little (1867) – Paul Barnes and Dave Foster (Commercial Type, 2014)

ABCDEFGHIJKLMNOPQRSTUVWX YZ&abcdefghijklmnopqrstuvwxyz¶ 1ı234567890ı234567890{[(.,;:!?*)]}

Paul Barnes and Dave Foster (n.d.) designed Marr Sans based on a few lines of a grotesque in three sizes and only one weight from the 1871 type specimen of James Marr & Co. in Edinburgh, successors to Alexander Wilson & Sons. What caught their attention was that the type, named Sans Serif No. 10 and shown in Pica, Long Primer, and Brevier sizes, had a lowercase and oldstyle figures, something not common at that time. Furthermore, the type was fascinating for its **g**, which in some sizes had a closed loop and in others was open. Out of these meager beginnings, they fabricated a full family of seven weights.

Nearly two years after Barnes and Foster completed the design of Marr Sans, they discovered that Sans Serif No. 10 was not an original Scottish design, but was in fact a copy of an American design called Gothic No. 4.

The 1867 specimen book of Farmer, Little & Co., a type-foundry in New York City, shows Gothic No. 4 in the same three sizes as Sans Serif No. 10, complete with oldstyle figures and the same varying form of **g**. Similar typefaces have been found by type critic Stephen Coles in specimen books of the Boston Type Foundry (where it is called Gothic No. 5), Bruce Foundry and Cincinnati Type Foundry from the 1860s, solidifying the source of Marr Sans as a distinctly American design.

However, none of this revised history has any bearing on the design of Marr Sans. Barnes and Foster have significantly redrawn most of the available characters from the Marr & Co. specimen to make them more harmonious and consistent, while retaining some of their funkiness. Most importantly, they settled on the quirky open loop **g**.

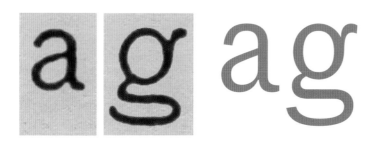

COMPARISON: **a**, **g** from Gothic No. 4 (Farmer, Little & Co.) vs. Marr Sans.

Grotesque No. 9

BIRKENHEAD
River Steamers

60 Point   5 A, 10 a; about 25 lb.

INVESTIGATION
Modern Equipment

48 Point   7 A, 14 a; about 24 lb.

HANDSOME POSTER
Provincial Dairy Farms

36 Point   12 A, 24 a; about 22 lb.

BEETHOVEN SYMPHONIES
Musicians Publishing Company

Bureau Grotesque Three Seven | Stephenson, Blake & Co. – David Berlow (Font Bureau, 1989)

ABCDEFGHIJKLMNOPQRSTUVWXYZ&abcde fghijklmnopqrstuvwxyzfifl1234567890 {[(.,;:!?*)]}¶

Late 19th-century and early 20th-century British sans serifs, called grotesques (or grots for short), are much more idiosyncratic than the homogenized sans serifs that have dominated graphic design since the rise of Univers and Helvetica at the end of the 1950s. The best of these were issued by P.M. Shanks & Sons and Stephenson, Blake & Co.

Magazine art director Roger Black discovered Stephenson, Blake & Co.'s Grotesque no. 9 (in a VGC phototypositor version) during his first job as an art director at a Los Angeles newspaper in 1972. As art director at *Newsweek* in 1985 he commissioned Jim Parkinson to draw a heavied-up version of Grotesque No. 9 to match the weight of Impact, the typeface used by the previous art director. Parkinson's design became known as Newsweek No. 9.

Four years later Black shared his passion for the Stephenson Blake grots with his Font Bureau partner David Berlow (b. 1954) who created the original Bureau Grotesque family. The first member to be drawn was Bureau Grotesque Thirty Seven, based on Grotesque No. 9, which, despite its 19th-century appearance, does not show up in a Stephenson, Blake & Co. specimen book until 1915.

The Stephenson, Blake & Co. grots are distinctive for their inward turned curves, curled tail on **Q**, sharply angled ear on **g**, and hooked arm on **r**. Berlow's original Bureau Grotesque family sticks very closely to the originals, keeping all of these warm and charming features. Since 1989 it has been greatly expanded, rationalized, and renumbered by other Font Bureau staff members. Members of the original family are shown below.

OPPOSITE: Grotesque No. 9 from *Printing Types: Borders, Initials, Electros, Brass Rules, Spacing Material, Ornaments* (Sheffield: Stephenson, Blake & Co., 1924).
COMPARISON (ABOVE RIGHT): **G**, **g** from Grotesque No. 9 vs. Bureau Grotesque Three Seven. (BELOW): Bureau Grotesque family.

Schelter Grotesk

No. 6032. 6 Cicero (72 Pkte.).† Mit Ziffern. 8 a 4 A = ¹/₁ Satz ca. 23 kg.

Gloriola

No. 6024. Mittel (14 Pkte.).†* 52 a 22 A = ¹/₁ Satz ca. 5,8 kg.

Christliche VORKÄMPFER im Mittelalter
2 INSTRUMENTISTES 4

No. 6031. 5 Cicero (60 Pkte.).† Mit Ziffern. 10 a 6 A = ¹/₁ Satz ca. 24 kg.

Musikalia

No. 6025. Tertia (16 Pkte.).†* 40 a 16 A = ¹/₁ Satz ca. 6,2 kg.

Bildwerke GRIECHISCHER Meister
TRIBUNAL 23 MADONNA

No. 6029. 3 Cicero (36 Pkte.).† 14 a 6 A = ¹/₁ Satz ca. 10,4 kg.

Critical 5 Notice
EDITION

Der Guss dieser Schriften ist auf systematische Unterlegbarkeit der einzelnen Grade unter einander berechnet.

6 Cicero, 5 Cicero, and Tertia Breite halbfette Grotesk from *Probensammlung J. G. Schelter & Giesecke* (Zweite Folge) (Leipzig, 1894), p. 545.

FF Bau Medium and Bold | Breite halbfette Grotesk (J.G. Schelter & Geisecke, 1886) – Christian Schwartz (FontShop, 2002)

ABCDEFGHIJKLMNOPQRSTU
VWXYZ&abcdefghijklmnopqrstu
vwxyz1234567890{[(.,;:!?*)]}¶

ABCDEFGHIJKLMNOPQRS
TUVWXYZ&abcdefghijklmno
pqrstuvwxyz1234567890
{[(.,;:!?*)]}¶

The most commonly used sans serif typeface at the Bauhaus was not Futura or Akzidenz Grotesk as one might expect, but Schelter Grotesk from the J.G. Schelter & Giesecke foundry in Leipzig. The first member of the Schelter Grotesk family was the Breite halbfette (wide medium) weight, which appeared in an 1886 catalogue. But the weight that the Bauhaus preferred was the Breite fette (wide bold), which does not show up in Schelter & Giesecke specimens until after 1894. That heftier type, as seen in Bauhaus publications and ephemera, inspired Christian Schwartz to design Bau, whose name is an homage to the famed design school.

Some of the features of Schelter Grotesk which Schwartz liked—and that had been erased by the neo-grotesques which emerged in the 1950s—are the angled endings of curved strokes, the double-story **g**, the **t** with an angled top, and the presence of oldstyle figures. Bau is not as slick as Helvetica or Univers, but neither is it as funky as the Stephenson Blake grots (see pp. 194–195).

COMPARISON: **G**, **a** from Breite halbfette Grotesk vs. FF Bau Medium.

Venus

V

Condensed

Extended

Regular

s

Classic Grotesque Pro Semibold | Venus Grotesk (Bauer, 1907) and Monotype Grotesque (Monotype Corporation, 1926) – Rod McDonald (Monotype, 2012)

ABCDEFGHIJKLMNOPQRSTUVWX YZ&ABCDEFGHIJKLMNOPQRSTUVWXY z&aɑbcdeeffgghijkllmnopqrstuvwx yyz11234567890112345678890 {[(.,;:!?*)]}¶

Monotype Grotesque (1926), the company's most durable sans serif alongside Gill Sans, was heavily used in the 1950s and 1960s by Swiss designers as a text companion to Akzidenz Grotesk and by English designers seeking to appear modern. The design has never been attributed to anyone, probably because the family was based on Berthold's Ideal Grotesk which, in turn, was a copy of Bauer's Venus Grotesk, both issued at the turn of the century. Thus, when Rod McDonald sought to revise Monotype Grotesque, he found himself instead reviving the German faces, especially Venus.

Venus is traditionally dated to 1907 and attributed to Bauer, but the design originated with Flinsch. Ideal Grotesk can be traced back to 1908. In their lighter weights, the two typefaces are virtually identical with

the strokes of the former but with more modulation and more sharply angled terminals. They share a number of distinctive, almost quirky, features: high waists on capitals such as **E** and **R**, tall **t** with an angled top, and **a** with a large bowl. Some of these features were toned down in Monotype Grotesque No. 215 (regular) and McDonald, who was not trying for an historical revival, has toned them down even more in Classic Grotesque. His goal was to make Classic Grotesque a text face rather than a display face.

McDonald modeled the light weights on Venus and the bold ones on Ideal Grotesk. He included small capitals, oldstyle figures, and a few of the unusual characters of those types (e.g., descending **f** and **u**-shaped **y**) as alternates.

OPPOSITE: Cover of a Venus specimen from Bauer Alphabets, Inc.
COMPARISON (ABOVE): **R, a** from Venus specimen and Classic Grotesque Semibold.

DIN 1451

DIN 1451 Beiblatt 3

Normschriften
Engschrift Mittelschrift Breitschrift
mit Hilfsnetz gemalt   Hilfsnetz für Malschablonen
Beispiele

Fette Engschrift

Innerhalb eines Wortes   Alleinstehend

abcdefghijklmnopqrstuvwxl

yzßäöü&.,-:;!?") 1234567890

ÄÖÜABCDEFGHIJKLMNOPQRST

UVWXYZ

Fette Mittelschrift

abcdefghijklmnopqrs

tuvwxyzßäöü&.,-:;!?")

1234567890ÄÖÜABC

DEFGHIJKLMNOPQR

FF DIN Bold (DIN 1451, 1936) – Albert-Jan Pool (FontShop, 1995)

ABCDEFGHIJKLMNOPQRSTUVWXY Z&abcdefghijklmnopqrstuvwxyz 1234567890{[(.,;:!?*)]}

DIN (Deutsche Industrie Normen) is an offspring of the trend at the turn of the 20th century toward standardization in industry, particularly in the recently unified Germany. In 1883, the Royal Prussian Railways published a master drawing showing a blocky, slightly condensed alphabet in outline and shaded outline versions intended for use on train coaches. In 1905, the railroad issued a new master drawing with outline letters that were lighter but more condensed.

To meet the need for standardized lettering on engineering and mechanical drawings, the Committee on Drawings of the Normenaus-schuß der Deutschen Industrie (Standardization Committee of the German Industry), issued DIN 16—a sloped handwritten block script—in 1919. The standardization movement reached the printing industry in 1926 when the members of the Standardization Committee of the Graphic Industry proposed that all printing offices in Germany should be equipped with a standardized printing type, preferably sans serif in design. The Committee on Type, founded the following year, extended the idea to a set of harmonized typefaces for engraving and lettering as well as printing that were not completed until 1931 when a "pre-norm" version was released as DIN 1451. The alphabet was only intended for signage due to opposition within the printing industry to a standardized typeface.

DIN 1451 was finalized in 1936 in three widths with the condensed version (DIN Engschrift) based on the 1905 Royal Prussian Railways alphabet. It became the official German typeface for motorway signage, street signs, license plates, and even wayfinding systems in bomb shelters. It was also used as a model for engraving.

FF DIN by Albert-Jan Pool (b.1960) is based on DIN 1451. An alternative interpretation is DIN Next by Akira Kobayashi and Sandra Winter.

ers ers ers

OPPOSITE: DIN 1451 Fette Engschrift and Fette Mittelschrift alphabet sheet with unit widths (1931).
COMPARISON (ABOVE): **e**, **r**, **s** from DIN 1451 | FF DIN Bold | DIN Next.

Highway Gothic

The Standard Alphabets for Traffic Control Devices, six series of mechanically drawn "gothic-style" alphabets (of varying widths—caps only—labeled A through F) were prepared by the Public Roads Administration (later the Federal Highway Administration) during World War II, initially for signs on the Pentagon road network. In 1949–1950 Series E Modified, along with a lowercase alphabet, was developed by the California Department of Transportation for use on highways. The two alphabets—usually credited to engineer Ted Forbes (1902–1992)—were paired as the basis of a national signage standard in 1958 with the publication of the AASHTO signing and marking manual for the new Interstate Highway System. Colloquially known as Highway Gothic, the FHWA series of alphabets have been the face of the American motoring landscape for nearly sixty years.

Highway Gothic is distinctive for its tall x-height, diagonally sheared ascenders, stubby single-case **g**, and **E** with a short mid-stroke. With its ubiquity, it is the embodiment of the vernacular letter. This feature attracted Tobias Frere-Jones, who in the early 1990s sought to turn Series E Modified into a proper typeface for printing purposes. The result was Interstate, an homage that is nearly as common as its model.

Overall, Interstate is smoother and better balanced—wider in the capitals but narrower in the lowercase—than Highway Gothic, thus making it more legible. Yet the quirkiness of the original has been retained.

Golden State Freeway in California (early 1950s).

Interstate | Highway Gothic [FHWA Series E] (Ted Forbes, Public Roads Administration, 1949 / 1952) –
Tobias Frere-Jones (Font Bureau, 1993)

ABCDEFGHIJKLMNOPQRSTUVWX
YZ&abcdefghijklmnopqrstuvwxyz
1234567890{[(.,;:!?*)]}

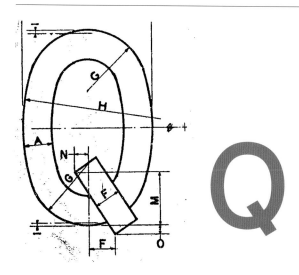

COMPARISON (TOP): Construction diagram for **Q** from *Standard Alphabets for Highway Signs* by the *Joint Committee on Uniform Traffic Control Devices* (Washington, DC: Department of Commerce, Bureau of Public Roads, 1952) and **Q** from Interstate.
COMPARISON (BOTTOM): **d, g** from contemporary interstate highway sign vs. Interstate.

Helvetica

C.20   Juni 57   C.16   22. AUG. 1957

Dampfschiffahrten

Dampfschiffahrten

AMERIKA-DIENST

AMERIKA-DIENST

Stoffe in bester Qualität

Stoffe in bester Qualität

DEUTSCHE TEXTILIEN

DEUTSCHE TEXTILIEN

Akz. Jr.

C.14

Nach Prüfung aller sonst noch bestehender Groteskschriften haben wir in Zusammenarbeit mit maßgebenden Graphikern und Typographen diese neue zeitlose Grotesk entwickelt.

Nach Prüfung aller sonst noch bestehender Groteskschriften haben wir in Zusammenarbeit mit maßgebenden Graphikern und Typographen diese neue zeitlose Grotesk entwickelt.

Fastest way to start a sale

Fastest way to start a sale

SYMBOLS OF ELEGANCE

SYMBOLS OF ELEGANCE

A?

C.24

Carte d'Identité

Carte d'Identité

PARIS / ROUEN

PARIS / ROUEN

A 9

C.36   26 NOV. 1957

Medinaceli

Medinaceli

HACIENDA

HACIENDA

A Gr.

C.28   26 NOV. 1957

Radiumbäder

Radiumbäder

BAUHAUS 15

BAUHAUS 15

Der Stand der Fernsehtechnik

Der Stand der Fernsehtechnik

SPORTBERICHT DER WOCHE

SPORTBERICHT DER WOCHE

C.12

Für die Technik ist die Erschließung neuer Energiequellen von besonderer Bedeutung

Für die Technik ist die Erschließung neuer Energiequellen von besonderer Bedeutung

ENERGIEGEWINNUNG AUS ATOMKERNEN

ENERGIEGEWINNUNG AUS ATOMKERNEN

C.8

Fremdsprachliche Lehrbücher sind nur Hilfsmittel, denn unmittelbarer

Fremdsprachliche Lehrbücher sind nur Hilfsmittel, denn unmittelbarer

REISEBÜRO ATLANTIS 234567890

REISEBÜRO ATLANTIS 34567890

C.10

19. FEB. 1958

Le programme du lundi de Pâques comportait deux épreuves d'obstacles, l'une plus importante et plus difficile que l'autre, mais présentant toutes les deux PRÉVISION POUR TOUTE LA FRANCE ET L'ITALIE

programme du lundi de Pâques comportait deux reuves d'obstacles, l'une plus importante et plus ficile que l'autre, mais présentant toutes les deux ÉVISIONS POUR TOUTE LA FRANCE ET L'ITALIE

2. MAI 1958

17. JAN. 1958

Blant de mange Lofotfilmer noterer vi Lofotliv, tatt opp etter initiativ av Norsk

Blant de mange Lofotfilmer noterer vi Lofotliv, tatt opp etter initiativ av Norsk

VINTERSPORTSSTEDER I TYSKLAND

VINTERSPORTSSTEDER I TYSKLAND

2. MAI 1958

Neue Haas Grotesk Display Medium | Neue Haas Grotesk (Max Miedinger, Haas, 1957) – Christian Schwartz
(Font Bureau, 2011)

ABCDEFGHIJKLMNOPQRRSTUVW XYZ&aabcdefghijklmnopqrstuvwxyz ff1234567890{[(.,;:!?*)]}¶

In 1956 Eduard Hoffmann (1892–1980), manager of the Haas typefoundry near Basel, gave Max Miedinger (1910–1980) the task of designing a new sans serif that would be an improvement on Akzidenz Grotesk, then the preferred sans serif of the new generation of modernist graphic designers in Switzerland. He closely supervised Miedinger's efforts, which resulted in the typeface Neue Haas Grotesk, the first weights of which were released in 1957. In 1960 the Stempel foundry, which owned a financial stake in Haas and German Linotype, rechristened the typeface Helvetica and adapted it for machine composition. By the middle of the decade it was available for sale in the United States and England and soon thereafter it began its meteoric rise in popularity. Although not the most widely used typeface in the world—that honor goes to Times Roman—Helvetica is undoubtedly the most widely known.

However, the current digital incarnation of Helvetica is not the real thing. Small changes to letters made as it was converted first to phototype, then larger ones as the family was revamped in 1983 and renamed Neue Helvetica, and finally additional small changes as the latter was converted to the PostScript format, have all combined to erode its original personality. Neue Haas Grotesk by Christian Schwartz is a revival of the original foundry design by Hoffmann and Miedinger, including two forms of **a** (with and without a tail), and an alternate straight-legged **R** only rarely seen before. Other than these alternates, the differences between Neue Haas Grotesk and Helvetica are not easily noticeable in an alphabet showing. The superiority of Neue Haas Grotesk is readily apparent, though, when text settings are compared.

GRR GR GR

OPPOSITE: Page (22 August 1957) from a journal kept by Eduard Hoffmann detailing the development of Neue Haas Grotesk, p. 19.
COMPARISON (ABOVE): Haas Grotesk Display Medium | Neue Helvetica Medium | AG Oldface Medium.

Eurostile

AABBCCDDEEF
FGGHHIIJJKKLL
MMNNOOPPQQ
RRSSTTUUVVX
XYYZZWWaabb
ccddeeffgghhiijjkk
llmmnnooppqqrrs
sttuuvvxxyyzzww
112233445566

Detail of Eurostile Serie Tonda Neretta Larga and Serie Tonda Nera Larga from a Società Nebiolo Torino specimen (1962).

Eurostile Next LT Pro Semibold Extended | Eurostile (Aldo Novarese, Nebiolo, 1962) – Akira Kobayashi
(Linotype, 2008)

ABCDEFGHIJKLMNOPQ RSTUVWXYZ&ABCDEFGH IJKLMNOPQRSTUVWXYZ&ab cdefghijklmnopqrstuvwxy z1234567890123456789 0{[(.,;:!?*)]}

Alessandro Butti (1893–1959) designed the all-capitals Microgramma as a titling face for Nebiolo in 1952. Roughly a decade later, Aldo Novarese (1920–1995), his former assistant who had taken over as head of the foundry's Studio Artistico, updated Microgramma, equipping it with a lowercase and extending the family to four weights. He also gave it a new name: Eurostile. Although never as popular as its contemporaries Univers and Helvetica, Eurostile, with its squarish shape (especially in the largo [wide] version) reminiscent of a television screen, became emblematic of the Space Age.

Akira Kobayashi has revived Eurostile as Eurostile Next and refurbished it for the Internet Age. He wisely refrained from designing italics and instead focused on adding weights and widths—along with small capitals and matching small lining figures. Kobayashi improved the distinctive "television screen" shape of the letters, but the only clearly discernible change to individual letters is a shifting of the tail of **Q** slightly downward to a more familiar position.

COMPARISON: **G, t** from Eurostile Nera Larga vs. Eurostile Next.

Geometric Sans Serifs

At the same time that the advocates of the new typography of the 1920s were trumpeting the virtues of grotesque types, several were also attempting to create a more rational and purer sans serif, one based on the simple geometric forms of the circle, triangle, and square. Experimental alphabets (as opposed to actual typefaces) in this vein were offered by Max Burchartz (1887–1961) in 1924, Herbert Bayer (1900–85) in 1925, Jan Tschichold in 1929, Kurt Schwitters (1887–1948) in 1927, Karel Teige (1900–51) in 1930, and others. But the two men who finally succeeded at creating viable geometric sans serif typefaces were not part of this younger generation of typographers.

Erbar Grotesk (1926) was designed by Jakob Erbar (1878–1935) for Ludwig & Mayer and Futura (1927) by Paul Renner (1878–1956) for Bauer. Although there is much argument over which was designed first (as opposed to released first) there is no doubt that Futura has been the more influential. Futura's success—which was virtually instantaneous—was due to several factors. Not only was it better designed than Erbar in the sense that it was geometrically purer (partly because Renner based the capitals on classical proportions rather than industrial ones), but it benefited from the marketing savvy and distribution clout of Bauer. Its name alone was brilliant.

Futura was promoted as "die Schrift unserer Zeit" (the typeface for our time) in specimens that showed a man—dressed in the garb of the new "visual engineer" envisioned by El Lissitzky (1890–1941) rather than that of a compositor—assembling advertisements in the manner of the new typography by cutting and pasting. Bauer had an office in New York to bring the type to the attention of American magazines and advertising agencies, which was very important in the metal era when Anglo-American and Continental types had different height to paper sizes.

Futura was quickly followed by a parade of competitors in Germany, across the Continent and even in England and America: Elegant Grotesk, Super Grotesk, Neuzeit Grotesk, Kabel, Nobel, Semplicità, Gill Sans, Granby, Vogue, Twentieth Century, Bernhard Sans, Goudy Sans, Metro, and more. Within three years the geometric sans serif had shoved aside the grotesque as the most popular form of sans serif, equally at home in designs inspired by the new typography and in Art Deco.

OPPOSITE: Detail of *Mostra della Rivoluzione Fascista* (1933) poster by C. V. Testi.

FUTURA

die Schrift unserer Zeit
BEGLEITE
das Bild unserer Zeit

It spread beyond the printed page to grace architecture and monuments from Fascist Italy to capitalist New York.

Several of the typefaces designed to compete with Futura consciously strove to temper its geometry with some "humanist" elements taken from broad-pen calligraphy or oldstyle typefaces. In this vein were Kabel by the calligrapher Rudolf Koch, Gill Sans by the sculptor Eric Gill, and Metro by W. A. Dwiggins (1880–1956). But in the end all three were forced to succumb to the full geometric aesthetic with the addition of alternate characters designed to be more in harmony with those of Futura. The typeface that best represents this urge to be simultaneously like Futura and not like Futura is Vogue (1930) from Intertype. Designed for *Vogue* magazine and its art director M. F. Agha (1896–1978), but released to the trade, it eventually sported a bewildering array of alternates that allowed it to mimic not only Futura but also Kabel, Tempo, and the early version of Futura with the squared **m** and **n**!

The reign of the geometric sans serifs was brought to an end in the late 1950s by the release of the neo-grotesques Univers and Neue Haas Grotesk (Helvetica). Yet, Futura continues to be popular ninety years later.

OPPOSITE: Page from type specimen *Futura: die Schrift unserer Zeit* (Frankfurt am Main: Bauer'sche Geisserei, 1928).
ABOVE: Seal of the City of New York, Junior High School 265, Brooklyn (1957). Photograph by Paul Shaw, 2009.

bayer

variation

In the 1920s a number of modernist designers in Germany and Eastern Europe sought to create the perfect geometrically-based alphabet to fit the zeitgeist of the machine age. The most famous of these is the Universal Alphabet of Herbert Bayer, designed during his stint as a teacher of typography at the Bauhaus. Although the Universal Alphabet is ostensibly constructed from the basic geometric forms of circle, triangle and square, a considerable number of letters deviate from that ideal. For several years Bayer experimented with the Universal Alphabet, testing different stroke widths (weights) and letter widths as well as the form of difficult letters like **a**. The earliest designs are probably from 1924, but it was not until 1926 that his proposal was published as part of *Offset Buch und Werbekunst* (Bauhausbücher no. 8). All of the versions of the Universal Alphabet are unicase, reflecting Bayer's lifelong belief that capital letters were redundant.

Although the forms of the Universal Alphabet were used by Bayer and other members of the Bauhaus in various designs, such as the masthead of the German lifestyle magazine *die neue linie*, it was never an actual typeface until the digital era. P22 Bayer Universal (part of the P22 Bayer Set that also includes P22 Bayer Shadow and P22 Bayer Fonetik) by Denis Kegler (b. 1974) and Richard Kegler is based on the heavy 1925 design. It is missing the alternate **a** that Bayer contemplated. Figures and basic punctuation have been added. Architype Bayer by David Quay (b. 1948) and Freda Sack (b. 1951) is based on a condensed version (c. 1924) of the Universal Alphabet. There are alternates for **f, g, i, j** and **k**. Figures and punctuation have been added.

Drawing (1925) by Herbert Bayer for the Universal Alphabet.

P22 Bayer Universal | Universal Alphabet (Herbert Bayer, 1925) – Denis Kegler and Richard Kegler (P22, 1997)

abcdefghijklmnopqrstuvwxyz&
1234567890{[(.,;:!?*)]}

Architype Bayer | Universal Alphabet (Herbert Bayer, c.1924) – David Quay and Freda Sack (The Foundry, 1997)

abcdeffgghiijjkkklmnopqrsttuvwxyz&
1234567890[[(.,;:!?)]

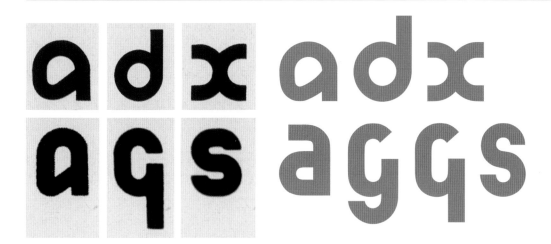

COMPARISON (ABOVE): **a**, **d**, **x** from Universal Alphabet (1925) by Bayer vs. P22 Bayer.
COMPARISON (BELOW): **a**, **g**, **s** from Universal Alphabet (c.1924) by Bayer vs. Architype Bayer.

Futura

Futura (1927) by Paul Renner was not the first geometric sans serif, being preceded by Erbar Grotesk (1926), but it is indisputably the most famous, the most influential, and the longest-lasting. The purity, simplicity and apparent perfection of Futura was arrived at by Renner after much experimentation and struggle over a two-year period, with many of the final forms benefiting from the input of Heinrich Jost (1889–1948), the art director at Bauer. Some of Renner's trial characters (such as r with a ball for the arm) briefly made it into the design released by Bauer, but most were discarded. Architype Renner by David Quay and Freda Sack is a revival of the experimental letters, including numerous alternates in all of their often strange imperfections, that were part of Renner's design process. (Note especially the multiple forms of a, e, g and r.)

Futura ND from Neufville Digital, the legal successors to Bauer, is based on the early releases of Futura, which included a few of Renner's experimental letters such as the square-topped m and n, as well as the original oldstyle figures. Also present are several other alternate forms (double-story a, l and t with curved feet) that Bauer tried out.

An invitation to a 1925 lecture by Paul Renner Munich entitled "Type: Dead or Alive?" set in an early version of Futura.

Architype Renner | Futura (Paul Renner, Bauer, 1925–1927) – David Quay and Freda Sack (The Foundry, 1997)

ABCDEFGHIJKLMNOPQRSTUVWXYZ&&
aɑɑᴀʌbcdeefggg̦g̦ghijklmɱnɳopqrrstuvwxyz
ﬀﬁﬂﬀﬁﬃ1234567890ı234567890
[(.,;:!?*)]

Futura ND Book | Futura (Paul Renner, Bauer, 1927) – Neufville Digital (1999)

ABCDEFGHIJJKLMMMNOPQRSTU
VWXYZ&aaɑbcdefgg̦hijjkllmɱnɳop
qrrsttuvwxyzﬀﬁﬂﬅﬃﬀﬂ1234567890
ı234567890{[(.,;:!?*)]}¶

COMPARISON: Architype Renner vs. Futura ND.

Nobel

Notre industrie du sucre avait

LA GALERIE DE PEINTURES

corps 28 no. 2516 minimum 10.25 kg kerf 2 100 / 75

Antieke griekse beelden

FRIESCHE FOLKLORE

corps 36 no. 2517 minimum 12 kg kerf 2 82 / 62

Guide des touristes

LES SARDINIERS

corps 48 no. 2518 minimum 15.50 kg kerf 2 64 / 48

De vierdaagse

ROTTERDAM

corps 60 no. 2519 minimum 21 kg kerf 2 48 / 36

Merveilleuse

corps 72 no. 2520 minimum 21.75 kg kerf 2 43 / 32

DTL Nobel | S. H. de Roos and Dick Dooijes (Lettergieterij Amsterdam, 1929) – Fred Smeijers and Andrea Fuchs
(Dutch Type Library, 1993)

ABCDEFGHIJKLMNOPQRSTUV WXYZ&abcdefghijklmnopqqrstuvw xyzfifl1234567890{[(.,;:!?*)]}◖◗

The Dutch response to the Futura phenomenon was
Nobel (1929), designed by S. H. de Roos (1877–1962)
and Dick Dooijes (1909–1998) for the Lettergieterij
Amsterdam. De Roos, the chief designer for the foundry
from 1903 until 1941, is best known as the designer of
Hollandsche Mediaeval (1912) and Erasmus Mediaeval
(1923), two typefaces that reflected his Arts and Crafts
aesthetic. Given those tastes, it is not surprising that
Nobel has a number of non-geometric traits such as the
E with a short vertex, the curved tail of **Q** and a single-
story **a**. Features like these make Nobel more Art Deco
than *neue typographie*.

DTL Nobel by Fred Smeijers and Andrea Fuchs
(b. 1966) is close to the original. A few subtle changes
have been made: the ascenders and **t** are slightly shorter;
A, **M** and **N** have pointed apexes; and the **S** is better balanced. Font Bureau has also issued a version of Nobel
designed by Tobias Frere-Jones in 1993 that is closer to
the De Roos/Dooijes original.

MMM
at at at at

OPPOSITE: Page from a Nobel specimen (Lettergieterij Amsterdam).
COMPARISON (ABOVE): Nobel (Amsterdam Type Foundry) | DTL Nobel | FB Nobel.

Metro

METRO
AND
METRO
No. 2

"THE MOST READABLE
OF THE SANS SERIFS"

Linotype's Metro series is an original sans serif face designed by W. A. Dwiggins, the eminent American illustrator and typographer, exclusively for Linotype. Metro No. 2 is distinguished from Metro by reason of substitute capital and lower case characters, yet each series may be converted into the other with minimum effort. Metro and Metro No. 2 are each available in a complete size range, from 6- to 36-point in Linotype matrices, with the A-P-L range of Metro No. 2 comprising 6- to 144-point. Each series is cut in four useful weights: Black, Medium, Lite and Thin. A companion Italic, in the Black, Medium and Lite weights, is a recent addition to the family in a range of two-letter sizes. Specimens, of all sizes and weights, are on following pages.

MERGENTHALER LINOTYPE COMPANY, BROOKLYN, N. Y. NEW YORK CITY, CHICAGO, SAN FRANCISCO, NEW ORLEANS, CANADIAN LINOTYPE, LIMITED, TORONTO · · · REPRESENTATIVES IN THE PRINCIPAL CITIES OF THE WORLD

◉ TRADE LINOTYPE MARK ◉

Metro Nova Pro | Metro and Metro No. 2 (W.A. Dwiggins, Mergenthaler Linotype, 1929–1932) – Toshi Omagari (Monotype, 2013)

AABCDEFGGHIJJKLMMNNOPQ
RSTUVVWWXYZ&&AABCDEFGGHI
JJKLMMNNOPQRSTUVVWWXYZ&&aab
cdeefgghijklmnopqrstuvvwwxyz
12233445566778899O
11234567890{[(.,;;:!?*)]}¶

In *Layout in Advertising* (1928), W. A. Dwiggins challenged American typefounders to design a sans serif with a decent lowercase. Soon thereafter, Mergenthaler Linotype took the bait and asked him to make such a face. The result was Metro in two duplexed weights, Metroblack and Metrothin, released in late 1929. These were followed by another duplexed pair, Metromedium and Metrolite. In designing the Metro family, Dwiggins, a product of the Arts and Crafts era, avoided geometric purity. He insisted on two-story forms for **a** and **g**; designed a peculiar cursive-looking **e**; gave **Q** a softly undulating tail; squared off the apexes and vertexes of **A**, **M**, **N**,**V** and **W**; and slightly angled the tops of ascenders. His intent was to make a "geometric" sans serif that could work as a text face.

Dwiggins' attempt to avoid copying the pure geometry of Futura failed. Futura's booming popularity in the United States forced Mergenthaler Linotype to ask him to redesign many of the letters to more closely mimic the German face. These new characters were issued in 1931 as Metro No. 2, with the original design being retroactively called Metro No. 1. Mergenthaler sold both designs, promoting them as interchangeable, but it was Metro No. 2 that became successful—so much so, that the original design was virtually forgotten.

Metro Nova by Toshi Omagari (b.1984) is a combination of Metro No. 1 and Metro No. 2, with the former as the default design. Proportions of letters have been adjusted to finally free them from the constraints of the duplexing system.

OPPOSITE: Metro and Metro No. 2 advertisement by Mergenthaler Linotype (1931).
COMPARISON (ABOVE): **gs** from Metro and Metro No. 2 vs. Metro Nova Pro.

Semplicità

DECURIONI
NORMANDOS
Blechdruckmaschine
DRUCKFACHLEUTE

The German pavilion at the 1930 Triennale in Milano, designed by Paul Renner and using his new type-face Futura, had a tremendous impact on modernist-inclined Italian graphic designers and architects. Geometrically constructed sans serif letters became the de facto style on Fascist buildings and monuments. Italian type foundries sought to make their own rational types. Semplicità, designed by Alessandro Butti in 1931 for Società Nebiolo, was a product of this Futura fever. It immediately became the default typeface for any Italian business seeking to appear up-to-date. It remained a staple of Italian graphic design and advertising into the 1960s.

Despite the influence of Futura, Semplicità is a very different design, with features that are deliberately more artisanal than mechanical. Ascenders are taller than capitals (a characteristic of oldstyle typefaces); the

bottoms of **U, a, d** and **u** are rounded off; the left portion of the crossbar of **f** and **t** has been deleted (and **f** descends); **A** has a very low crossbar while the midpoint of **E, F, K** and **R** is high. In short, Semplicità has personality.

Semplicità was little known outside of Italy until Patrick Griffin (b. 1970) revived it as Semplicita Pro. His design includes alternate letters to the distinctive ones created by Butti, small caps and oldstyle figures. Proportions of the capitals have been regularized. For these reasons, Claudio Piccinini (b. 1969), an Italian type designer who has researched Butti's work, has heavily critiqued the design as lacking the spirit of Butti's original, which he has eloquently described as, "Economical in means, elegant by necessity through its sobriety. Deliberately modern, despite its warmth and friendliness."

Details from *Semplicità Specimen* (Società Nebiolo Torino, N.D.).

Semplicita Pro | Semplicità (Alessandro Butti, Nebiolo, 1931) – Patrick Griffin (Canada Type, 2011)

AABCDEFGHIJJJKLMNOPQRSTU
VWXYZ&&aabcdefffghijjklmmnnop
qrstttuvwxyz{[(.,;:!?*)]}¶
1234567890₁₂₃₄₅₆₇₈₉₀

RaRa
ffff

COMPARISON (ABOVE): **R, a** from Semplicità (Nebiolo) vs. Semplicita Pro.
BELOW: Variant forms of **f** from Semplicita Pro.

Gotham City

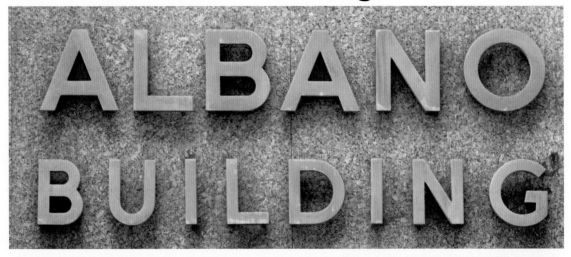

Gotham is the Futura of the 21st century, both in its machine-age aesthetics and in its unprecedented popularity. Its design grew out of sans serif inscriptions and signs on public buildings in New York dating from the New Deal era—but continuing in use through the 1960s—that Jonathan Hoefler saw on his daily walks in the city. These letters—which only existed as capitals—were geometric yet they did not look like Futura. Their widths were more uniform and less classical; bowls were larger; and midstrokes, crossbars, and junctions were positioned lower or higher than expected. Out of numerous architectural and signage samples Tobias

Frere-Jones distilled Gotham, adding a lowercase of his own devising, marked by a large x-height and a default single-story **a**.

Hoefler and Frere-Jones dubbed their design Gotham after the 19th-century nickname for New York. However, capital letters similar to those that inspired it can be found throughout the United States as well as in Europe, on government buildings and monuments erected in the period from the mid-1920s through the end of the 1950s, and on surviving commercial signs from that era. They were especially prevalent in Fascist Italy.

Gotham Medium | New York City signage (1930s–1960s) – Jonathan Hoefler and Tobias Frere-Jones
(Hoefler Type Foundry, 2000)

ABCDEFGHIJKLMNOPQQRSTU VWXYZ&aabcdefghijklmnopqr stuvwxyz112334567890 {[(.,;:!?*)]}¶

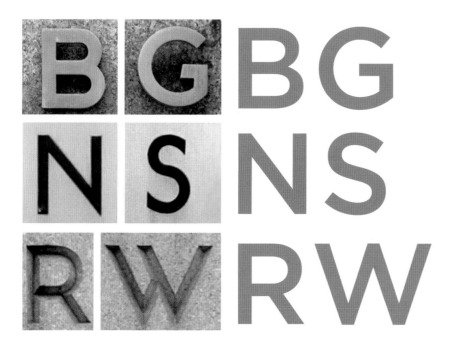

OPPOSITE: Details of three examples of geometric sans serif architectural lettering in New York City. TOP: The Albano Building (1928);
MIDDLE: New York City Criminal Courts Building (1941); BOTTOM: The Department of Health, City of New York (1935).
COMPARISON (ABOVE): B, G from Albano Building signage (TOP LINE); N, S from signage on New York City Criminal Courts Building
(MIDDLE LINE); R, W from New York City Department of Health building inscription (BOTTOM LINE) vs. Gotham Medium.

FASCIST ITALY

The Fascist era in Italy, from Mussolini's march on Rome in 1922 to his public execution in 1943, is marked typographically by a preference for sans serif capitals in a wide range of geometrically-influenced styles from the soberness of the Architettura razionale movement to the wild yet ingenious inventions of Art Deco travel posters and packaging. Mark Simonson (b. 1965) has gathered many of these letters—from the slender to the blocky—together as Mostra Nuova, a family of six weights. Essentially, Mostra Nuova is an anthology of geometric interpretations of the roman alphabet from the Art Deco era in Italy. Its numerous alternates shift across the range of weights, reflecting the solutions Fascist-era artists and designers applied to problems that arise as letters become bulkier and bulkier: midstrokes are rendered as triangles, crossbars are dramatically lowered, **S** becomes a narrow undulating line, the position of the tail of **Q** shifts about, and so on. All in all, Mostra Nuova is an evocation of a time and place rather than a revival of a specific group of letters.

Detail of a 1936 poster advertising the move of Sirtoli Lito, a Milanese printer. Designer unknown.

Mostra Nuova Regular | Mark Simonson (Mark Simonson Studio, 2009)

AAABCCDEEFFGGGGHIJKKLMMMMNOP
QQQQRRSSSSTUVWWXYYZ&
aabccdeefgghiijjkklmnopqrrssssstuuvwxyz3
1234567890{[(.,:::!?*)]}¶

Mostra Nuova Black | Mark Simonson (Mark Simonson Studio, 2009)

AAABCCDEEFFGGGGHIJKKLMMAM
NOPQQQQRRSSSSSSTUVWWXYYZ&
aabccdeefgghiijjkklmnopqrrssssst
uuvwxyz31234567890{[(.,:::!?*)]}

COMPARISON: Mostra Nuova Regular vs. Mostra Nuova Black.

LIBRI
MEDULLITUS
DELECTANT/
COLLOQUUNTUR/
CONSULUNT/
ET VIVA QUADAM
NOBIS ATQUE
ARGUTA
FAMILIARITATE
IUNGUNTUR

PETRARCA

1959

Humanist Sans Serifs

A year after the release of Neue Haas Grotesk and Univers, Stempel released Optima by Hermann Zapf, describing it as a typeface with the clarity of a classical roman letter and the precision of a grotesque sans serif. Zapf initially referred to it during development as a "neu-antiqua." Optima confused people because it lacked serifs, but contrary to the expectations built up over a century and a half of exposure to grotesques, it was not monolinear, nor did it even pretend to be. It had the same well defined stroke contrast that characterized oldstyle types. Consequently, some contemporary critics called it a serifless roman rather than a sans serif.

Just over a decade later Stempel released Syntax (1969) by Hans Eduard Meier (1922–2014), its last foundry type. Meier intended his design to be a sans serif equivalent of a French Oldstyle design. A decade later, Sumner Stone, writing about it for *Fine Print*, described it as a humanist sans serif, thus establishing a new category of typeface. Optima was quickly added to the new category, as were some older types such as Gill Sans.

Stone's interest in Syntax was a personal one. It was an inspiration for ITC Stone Sans (1987) as well as for Lucida Sans (1985), designed by his college classmate Charles Bigelow (b. 1945) in collaboration with Kris Holmes (b. 1950). With the release of these faces—which were among the first to have serif companions—the humanist sans serif category got an immediate boost. Since then numerous additional designs have been added to it, especially as contemporary designers create super families of matching serif and sans types (e.g., FF Scala [1991] and FF Scala Sans [1993]).

The most important aspect of humanist sans serif types is that they have proportions and an underlying structure based on oldstyle typefaces. Capitals have varying widths, and x-heights tend to be smaller than those of grotesques. There is no beard on **G**, the strokes of **K** meet at a single point, **M** is often splayed, **Q** has a diagonal tail, **R** has a diagonal leg, **a** and **g** are double-story, and **y** often has a curved tail. In some designs, strokes have angled terminals. Whether or not letters have contrasting thick/thin strokes, like Optima or Pascal, is not essential.

OPPOSITE: A pencil drawing for a medal in cast silver by Hermann Zapf (1959).

Gill Sans

ABCDEFGH
IJKLMNOP
QRRSTUVW
XYZ& .,:;-"'!?¶
£II23456

Gill Sans (1928) was designed by the sculptor, illustrator, engraver, lettercarver and polemicist Eric Gill for the Monotype Corporation as a British answer to the Futura phenomenon. It was quickly taken up by British printers, designers and advertising agencies to the point where today it is perceived as the national typeface of Britain. Its popularity required Monotype to add numerous weights and widths to the family, many with minimal or no input from Gill. In addition, in order to increase sales to Continental customers Monotype felt compelled to alter many of the typeface's most distinctive characters (e.g., **a** and **g**) to make them more resemble Futura.

The result of decades of fussing with Gill Sans left the family in a disorganized state. In 2015 Monotype Imaging, the descendant of the Monotype Corporation, decided to clean things up with the commission of Gill Sans Nova carried out by George Ryan (b. 1950). Ryan's redesign restored some letters to their original forms, altered others to be more harmonious, but kept many of the variant characters that had accumulated over time. Gill Sans Nova is thus a smorgasbord of many of the previous iterations of the typeface, allowing users to choose the version they prefer: e.g., **a** with a tail or without, single-story or double-story, and so on.

Detail of Trial No. 2 of Gill Sans Titling Caps (9 April 1929) with letters retouched by Eric Gill (18 February 1930).

Gill Sans Nova Book | Gill Sans (Eric Gill, Monotype, 1928) – George Ryan (Monotype, 2015)

AABCDEFGHIJJKLMMNNOPQRSTUU
VVVWWXYZ&ABCDEFGHIJKLMNOPQRSTUV
wxyzaaabbcddefgggghijklmnoppqqrstuv
wxyzff1I234567890₁₂₃₄₅₆₇₈₉₀
{[(.,;:!?*)]}¶☜☜☞

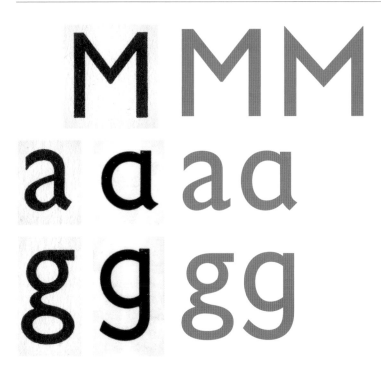

COMPARISON: **M**, **a**s, **g**s from various versions of Gill Sans vs. Gill Sans Book Nova.

Optima

36 p Optima Nr. 5699

Zurichtung vom C nachprüfen

ABCDEFGHIJKLMNOPQRS

TUVWXYZ

diese Partie ist zu leicht   *Rundung verbogen ebenso beim Œ und Q*   *jetzt ok*

ÆŒÇÄÖÜÅØ & MN

verbogen   *Bogen nicht gut*

abcdefghijklmnopqr   *r ev. etwas breiter*

Bogen oben zu flach und Übergang zu hart

stuvwxyz chckfffiflftß

obere Partie zu leicht

|a|b|c|d|e|f|g|h|i|j|k|l|m|n|o|p|q|r| *?*

a rund |s|t|u|v|w|x|y|z| æœçäöü   *Bogen schlecht*

åøáâàéêèëíîìïíjóôòúûù

Ligatur ij in der Weite nachprüfen

.,:;!?„"-'—»«// * † [(§)]

* *Zurichtung der Ziffer 4?*

$1234*567890 £

The Museum of Modern Art

D. Stempel AG 8.11.1958

12.11.1958

Zurichtung vom M nachprüfen

Optima Nova | Optima (Hermann Zapf, Stempel, 1958) – Hermann Zapf and Akira Kobayashi (Linotype, 2002)

ABCDEFGHIJKLMNOPQRSTUVWXY Z&abcdefghijklmnopqrstuvwxyz& abcdefghijklmnopqrstuvwxyz fifl 1234567890123456789O{[(.,;:!?*)]}ç

Optima (1958) was designed by Hermann Zapf following a trip to Italy in 1950. In florence he was inspired by modulated sans serif lettering found on a number of floor tombs in Santa Croce. Originally intending to create a display face, Zapf added a lowercase of his own invention upon the advice of Monroe Wheeler (1899–1988), Director of Exhibitions and Publications at the Museum of Modern Art in New York from 1941 to 1967. Upon its release, Optima puzzled many in the design world as it appeared to be neither a seriffed face nor a grotesque in the 19th-century manner. Described by some critics as a serif-less roman, it helped pioneer the creation of the humanist sans serif category.

The digital redesign of Optima as Optima Nova by Zapf was carried out with the aid of Akira Kobayashi. In the roman most of the alterations are subtle, such as the redrawing of **f** to reflect the lack of kerning restrictions and the addition of a thickened terminal to the upper curve of **a** and a change in the angle of the tail on **Q**. Zapf and Kobayashi made greater revisions to the italic, increasing its angle of inclination and adding cursive letters (e.g., **a**, **e**, **f**, **g** and **l**) to bring the face closer to a true italic instead of an oblique roman. A condensed design and a titling face (see Optima Nova Titling, pp. 30–31) were also added to the family.

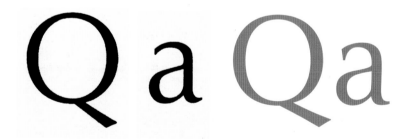

OPPOSITE: 36 pt (Didot) Optima proof (8 November 1958) with annotations by Hermann Zapf (12 November 1958).
COMPARISON (ABOVE): **Q**, **a** from Optima (Stempel) vs. Optima Nova.

Syntax

ABCDEFGHIJKLMN
OPQRSTUVWXYZ
abcdefghijklmnopqrst
uvwxyz 1234567890

**ABCDEFGHIJKLMN
OPQRSTUVWXYZ
abcdefghijklmnopqrst
uvwxyz 1234567890**

Detail of a page from *Syntax-Antiqua* (Frankfurt-am-Main, D. Stempel AG, 1969).

LT Syntax | Syntax-Antiqua (Hans Eduard Meier, Stempel, 1969) – Hans Eduard Meier (Linotype Library, 2000)

ABCDEFGHIJKLMNOPQRSTUVWX
YZ&ABCDEFGHIJKLMNOPQRSTUVWXY
z&abcdefghijklmnopqrstuvwxyzfifl
1234567890123456789o{[(.,;:!?*)]}¶

Hans Eduard Meier spent nearly a decade and a half, from 1955 to 1969, perfecting the design that became Syntax, the last metal typeface issued by Stempel. When it was released, graphic design was just coming under the full dominance of Helvetica. Syntax, a sans serif with a structure inspired by Renaissance oldstyle types (e.g., Stempel Garamond) was out of step with the times and did not gain immediate favor. However, by the 1990s it had a devoted following.

Most early digital typefaces were simply copied directly from their phototype predecessor, which itself had been copied directly from a foundry version. Such copying failed to take into account the shift from metal types designed with optical adjustments for different sizes to film and pixel types, which were infinitely scalable. In the late 1990s Linotype began a concerted effort to redesign its most important legacy types from the ground up. Syntax was one of the first of the "optimized classic typefaces" in the Platinum Collection.

Meier welcomed the chance to revise Syntax since he felt the Stempel version had never fully matched his vision for the typeface. With LT Syntax he made major changes (widening **M** and giving **R** an open bowl) and minor tweaks (reshaping **g**). He also narrowed the italic and added more cursive qualities to some of the letters to make the typeface less of an oblique roman.

GMR a
GMR a

COMPARISON: **G**, **M**, **R**, **a** from Syntax-Antiqua (Stempel) vs. LT Syntax.

Scripts

Script types are usually defined as types that imitate cursive writing and divided into groups based on the tools used to make them: the broad-edged pen, the flexible pointed pen, and the brush. The broad-edged pen group includes chancery italic (though all other italics are excluded because of their status as companions to roman), ronde and bâtarde coulée; while the pointed pen group includes roundhand and Spencerian script. These are all formal scripts. Brush scripts, which vary widely, are informal; as are scripts based on handwriting. The four script typefaces in this chapter are a chancery italic, a roundhand, a Spencerian script and a script derived from 20th-century handwriting. Due to space limitations, there are no brush scripts.

Chancery italic is a 15th-century Renaissance script that is minimally sloped and, in its formal variety, has few joins. In contrast, roundhand and Spencerian are highly sloped and almost continuously joined. Both of these features present problems for transforming into type. The first typeface cut in imitation of roundhand scripts, that of Thomas Cottrell in 1774, dazzled contemporaries because of its joined appearance. He achieved this through close fitting of his letters.

Achieving the appearance of seamlessly joined letters intrigued and challenged 19th-century and 20th-century typefounders. To do so they kerned and ligatured letters and invented special type bodies that were winged, offset or angled. The most elaborate method devised to successfully mimic script in type was that of Firmin Didot in which Anglaise (the French name for roundhand) was broken down into components: parts of letters, letters, pairs of letters, and letters joined to parts of another letter. It was ingenious but impractical.

The ultimate solution, however, was to get rid of the metal type body altogether. That happened with the invention of phototype in the middle of the 20th century. Snell Roundhand (1965) by Matthew Carter, made for the Linofilm machine, was the first script to take advantage of the freedoms allowed by phototype. Finally, the advent of the OpenType font format in 1997, with its enormous glyph palette, followed by the release of Adobe InDesign, with contextual features (2003), has more than ever allowed type to look like script.

OPPOSITE: Detail of text composed in foundry Mistral. Note the sans serif letters below the type to aid the compositor in identifying each character..

Arrighi

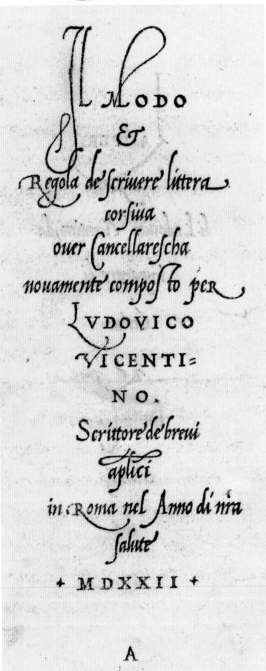

Ludovico Vicentino degli Arrighi was a scribe in the Vatican chancery. His renown as a calligrapher rests primarily on his authorship of *La Operina di Ludovico Vicentino, da Imparare di scrivere littera Cancellarescha* (1522), the first writing manual. His calligraphy was masterfully cut on wood in relief by Ugo da Carpi (c.1480–1520/1532).

P22 Operina by James Grieshaber (b.1967) recreates Arrighi's chancery italic, complete with ink squash and other blemishes, as it appears in *La Operina*. It comes in three flavors (Corsivo, Fiore and Romano) that were originally independent fonts before being combined into P22 Operina Pro in 2005. Romano has upright roman capitals and lining figures; Corsivo has swash capitals, elongated ascenders and descenders, and oldstyle figures; and Fiore is characterized by elaborate swash characters, including some figures. The capitals of Fiore have been extracted from Arrighi's text where they were designed to fit a specific context. All three P22 Operina subfonts have modern figures and punctuation.

ABOVE LEFT: Detail from f.1v of *La Operina di Ludovico Vicentino, da imparare di scrivere littera Cancellarescha* by Ludovico Vicentino degli Arrighi (Rome, 1522 [1524]).
COMPARISON (RIGHT): "Lvdo" from *La Operina* and P22 Operina.

P22 Operina Pro | Arrighi (*Il Modo*, 1522) – James Grieshaber (P22, 2003)

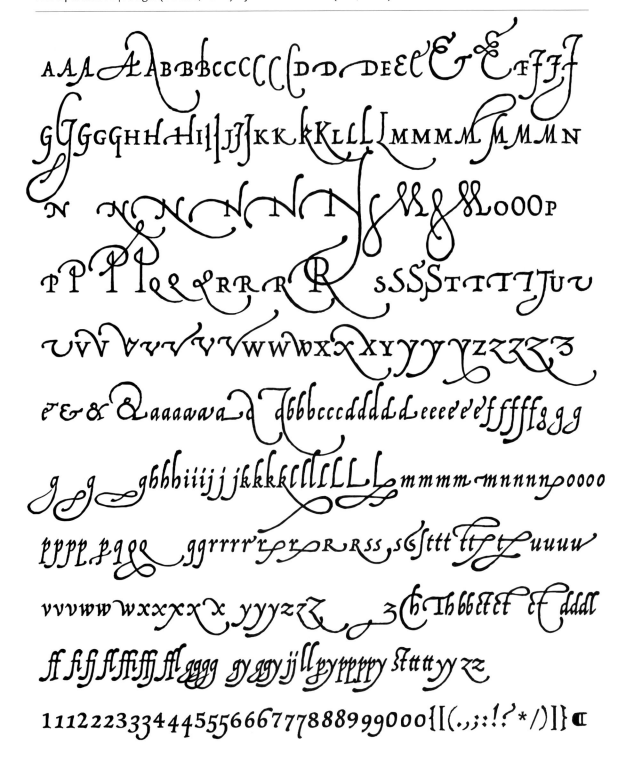

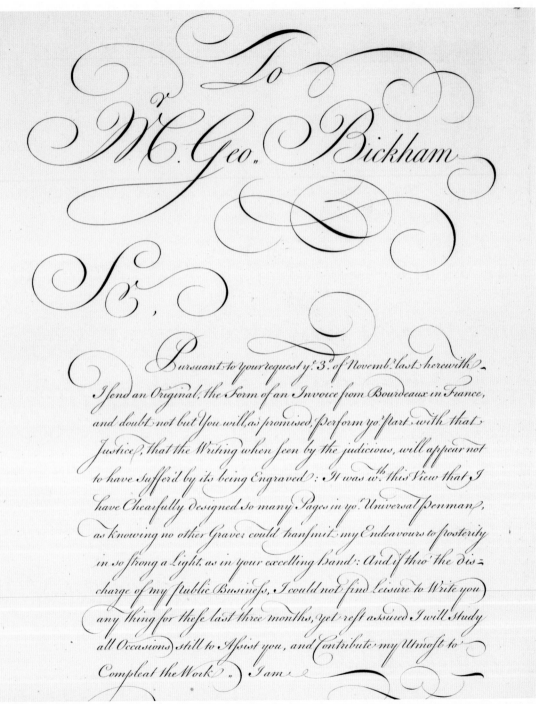

Bickham

To
Mr. Geo. Bickham

Sr,

Pursuant to your request yr 3. of Novembr last herewith, I send an Original, the Form of an Invoice from Bourdeaux in France, and doubt not but You will, as promised, perform yor part with that Justice, that the Writing when seen by the judicious, will appear not to have Sufferd by its being Engraved: It was wth this View that I have Chearfully designed So many Pages in yor Universal Penman, as knowing no other Graver could transmit my Endeavours to posterity in so strong a Light, as in your excelling hand: And if thro' the discharge of my publick Business, I could not find Leisure to Write you any thing for these last three months, yet rest assured I will Study all Occasions still to Assist you, and Contribute my Utmost to Compleat the Work. I am

Calligraphy by Joseph Champion (1739) engraved by George Bickham. From *The Universal Penman; or, The Art of Writing Made Useful...* by George Bickham (London: H. Overton, 1741).

Bickham Script Pro | George Bickham et al (*The Universal Penman*, 1741) – Richard Lipton (Adobe, 1997)

The Universal Penman is possibly the *sine qua non* of writing manuals. It was engraved in 52 parts by George Bickham (1684?–1758?) between 1733 and 1741. The book collects the work of twenty-five leading English writing masters of the day in 212 plates, 18 of which were by Bickham himself. Among the other writing masters displayed were John Bland (1702–1750) with five plates; William Kippax (1705–1755) with seven plates; Willington Clark (c.1715–1755) with 21 plates; Nathaniel Dove (1711–1754) with 27 plates; and Joseph Champion (1709–c.1768) with a whopping 47 plates. Although *The Universal Penman* includes a variety of writing styles, the dominant one is roundhand (today commonly known as copperplate script).

Bickham Script by Richard Lipton (b.1963), an accomplished calligrapher as well as type designer, has been synthesized from the various roundhand examples in *The Universal Penman*. It is not an exact replica as Lipton has filtered the work of the English writing masters through his own calligraphic sensibility. The full glyph palette of Bickham Script includes oversize swash capitals, regular swash capitals, small swash capitals, a lowercase with alternates with various degrees of swashiness, ligatures, flourishes designed to attach as beginnings or as endings to characters, independent ornaments, and, of course, figures and punctuation. It is a brilliant design that requires a high degree of typographic ability for its riches to be fully appreciated.

Madarasz

Louis Madarasz (1859–1910), who claimed to have originated the Coca-Cola swash script, was one of the greatest American penman of his time. He was especially celebrated for his "signature writing" in which the initial letters are accentuated with ornamentation and extra weight is added to selected strokes. Madarasz' style of pointed pen writing is a bolder version of the Spencerian tradition originated by Platt Rogers Spencer (1800–1864). Spencer, whose copybooks first appeared in the 1850s, and his followers advocated the achievement of faster writing speeds by reducing the number of loops and swashes, relegating such decorative effects to capitals and finial letters.

Alejandro Paul (b. 1972) based Burgues Script on samples of Madarasz' work gathered in *The Madarasz Book: The Secret of the Skill of Madarasz, His Philosophy and Penmanship Masterpieces* (1911), a tribute book published after his death. The font has multiple alternates for each capital, alternates for many of the lowercase letters, initial and finial swash letters, and loose flourishes. Burgues Script is a welcome alternative to the dominant roundhand style of formal script typefaces.

Detail of Plate Three from *The Madarasz Book: The Secret of the Skill of Madarasz, His Philosophy and Penmanship Masterpieces* (Columbus, Ohio: Zaner & Bloser, 1911).

Burgues Script | Louis Madarasz (1890s) – Alejandro Paul (Sudtipos, 2008)

Mistral

un homme écrit...

...et dans chaque signe,

sa main, singulière,

inscrit son émotion,

sa signature, son secret.

Gravés dans le métal,

ses mouvements témoignent

d'une conviction :

les **Scriptes** sont orateurs,

ils appellent

en marge des textes.

Leur timbre est celui

de la publicité.

Showing of Mistral from *Trois Scriptes* specimen book (Fonderie Olive, 1956).

ITC Mistral Light | Mistral (Roger Excoffon, Fonderie Olive, 1953) – Phill Grimshaw (ITC, 1997)

ABCDEFGHIJKLMNOPQRSTUVWXYZ&& ABCDEFG
HIJKLMNOPQRSTUVWXYZabcdefghijklmnopqrst
uvwxyz esfifl quthstffll om on oo 1234567890
1234567890[(.,;:!?*)]¶

Roger Excoffon (1910–1983) is best known as the designer of Mistral (1953), a script that broke new ground for the manner in which it managed to achieve the appearance of casual handwriting. In the era of metal type, this was no small feat. Creating script typefaces in metal was always difficult because the idea was inherently contradictory: the letters of scripts run together while the letters of metal type are discrete units. Excoffon, who based Mistral on his own handwriting, employed several strategies to hide the joins between letters without resorting to kerns. He varied the basic form of similar letters (and designed a stroke that, depending on its context, can be interpreted as an l, f or p); joined letters with varying degrees of angles and points of departure; aligned letters irregularly at base and top; included ligatures; and gave the letters a granular outline that print historian John Dreyfus claimed "prevented the eye from detecting awkward changes in direction of stroke." Fonderie Olive issued Mistral in a single weight.

When Phill Grimshaw revived Mistral the problems that Excoffon had to solve in designing it no longer existed. Grimshaw's only challenge was in keeping the lively spirit of the original. He invented a new light weight, but wisely refrained from creating new alternate letters or ligatures, restricting himself to adding small capitals and oldstyle figures.

COMPARISON: "question" from a Mistral specimen reproduced in *The Penrose Annual*, vol. 50 (1956) vs. ITC Mistral.

Selected Bibliography

GENERAL

Caflisch, Max. *Schriftanalysen*. St. Gall: Typotron, 2003. 2 vols.

Dowding, Geoffrey. *An Introduction to the History of Printing Types*. London: Wace & Company Ltd., 1961.

Johnson, A. F., et al. *Type Specimen Facsimiles*. London: Bowes & Bowes, 1963.

Kelly, Jerry. *Type Revivals: What are they? Where did they come from? Where are they going?* New York: The Typophiles, 2011.

Knight, Stan. *Historical Types: From Gutenberg to Ashendene*. New Castle, DE: Oak Knoll Press, 2012.

Lo Celso, Alejandro. "A Discussion on Type Revivalism." MA thesis, University of Reading, 2000.

Meggs, Philip B. and Roy McKelvey, eds. *Revival of the Fittest: Digital Versions of Classic Typefaces*. New York: RC Publications, 2000.

Mosley, James. *A Dictionary of Punchcutters for Printing Types*. Unpublished, 1999.

Sutton, James and Alan Bartram. *The Atlas of Type Forms*. London: Lund Humphries, 1968.

Updike, Daniel Berkeley. *Printing Types: Their History, Forms, and Use*. Cambridge, MA: The Belknap Press of Harvard University Press, 1966. Orig. pub. 1922. 2 vols.

INSCRIPTIONAL LETTERS

Catich, Edward M. *Letters Redrawn from the Trajan Inscription in Rome*. Davenport, IA: Catfish Press, 1961.

Gray, Nicolete. *A History of Lettering: Creative Experiment and Letter Identity*. David R. Godine, Publisher, 1986.

———. *Sans Serif and Other Experimental Lettering of the Early Renaissance*. New York and Seattle: LetterPerfect, 1997). Reprinted from *Motif* 5 (1960).

Re, Margaret et al. *Typographically Speaking: The Art of Matthew Carter*. Baltimore: Albin O. Kuhn Library & Gallery, University of Maryland, Baltimore County, 2002

Shaw, Paul, ed. *The Eternal Letter: Two Millennia of the Roman Classical Capital*. Cambridge, MA and London: The MIT Press, 2014.

Unger, Gerard. "Romanesque capitals in inscriptions" in *Typography Papers* 9 (2013).

BLACKLETTER

Bain, Peter and Paul Shaw, eds. *Blackletter: Type and National Identity: A Catalogue of the Exhibition* (*Printing History* 38/39 vol. XIX, no. 2 and vol. XX, no. 1, 1999).

Kapr, Albert. *Johann Gutenberg: The Man and His Invention*. Trans. Douglas Martin. Aldershot, England: Scolar Press, 1996.

Klingspor, Karl. *Über Schönheit von Schrift und Druck*. Frankfurt am Main: Georg Kurt Schauer, 1949.

Shaw, Paul. *The Calligraphic Tradition in Blackletter Type*. (*Scripsit* vol. 22, nos. 1 & 2, 1999).

Vervliet, H. D. L. *Sixteenth-Century Printing Types of The Low Countries*. Amsterdam: Menno Hertzberger & Co., 1968.

VENETIAN OLDSTYLE & ALDINE TYPES

Olocco, Riccardo. "I Romani di Francesco Griffo" in *Bibliologia* 7 (2012).

FRENCH OLDSTYLE TYPES

Argetsinger, Mark. "Adobe Garamond: A Review" in *Printing History* 26/27 vol. XIII, no. 2 and vol. XIV, no. 1, 1992.

Beaujon, Paul [Beatrice Warde]. "The 'Garamond' Types: A Study of XVI and XVII Century Sources Considered" in *The Fleuron* no. V (1926).

Beaujon, Paul [Beatrice Warde], ed. *The 1621 specimen of Jean Jannon*. Paris, 1927.

Lane, John A. "Garamond and His Roman Types" in *Garamond Premier Pro*. San Jose: Adobe Systems, 2005.

Slimbach, Robert. "The Making of Garamond Premier" in *Garamond Premier Pro*. San Jose: Adobe Systems, 2005.

Johnson, A. F. "The Italic Types of Robert Granjon" in *The Library*, 4th series, XXI (1941).

Vervliet, H. D. L. *Sixteenth-Century Printing Types of The Low Countries*. Amsterdam: Menno Hertzberger & Co., 1968.

———. *The Palaeotypography of the French Renaissance*. Leiden & Boston: Brill, 2008. 2 vols.

———. *French Renaissance Printing Types: A Conspectus*. London: The Bibliographical Society and The Printing Historical Society and New Castle, DE: Oak Knoll Press, 2010.

DUTCH OLDSTYLE TYPES

Haiman, György. *Nicholas Kis, a Hungarian Punch-cutter and Printer 1650–1702*. Budapest: Akadémiai Kiadó; San Francisco: Jack W. Stauffacher / The Greenwood Press, 1983.

Lane, John A.. "The Types of Nicholas Kis" in *Journal of the Printing Historical Society*, no. 18 (1984).

Smeijers, Fred. *Counterpunch: Making Type in the Sixteenth Century, Designing Typefaces Now*. London: Hyphen Press, 1996.

TRANSITIONAL TYPES

Ballus, Andreu et al. *Imprenta Real Fuentes de la Tipografía Española*. Madrid: Ministerio de Asuntos Exteriores y de Cooperación, 2009.

Enschedé, Charles. *Fonderies de Caractères et leur Matériel dans les Pays-Bas du XVe au XIXe Siècle*. Haarlem: Joh. Enschedé en Zonen, 1908.

Hutt, Allen. *Fournier: The Compleat Typographer*. Totowa, NJ: Rowman and Littlefield, 1972.

Jammes, André. *La Réforme de la Typographie Royale sous Louis XIV: Le Grandjean*. Paris: Editions Promodis, 1985. Orig. pub. 1961.

Lane, John. *The Enschedé Type Specimens of 1768 & 1773: Introduction and Notes*. Haarlem and Amsterdam: Stichting Museum Enschedé, The Enschedé Font Foundry and Uitgeverij de Buitenkant, 1993.

Mosley, James. *Le Romain du Roi: La Typographie au Service de l'État, 1702–2002*. Lyon: Musée de l'Imprimerie, 2002.

Pardoe, F. E. *John Baskerville of Birmingham Letter-Founder & Printer*. London: Frederick Muller Limited, 1975.

NEOCLASSICAL

De Pasquale, Andrea. *La Fucina dei Caratteri di Giambattista Bodoni*. Parma: Monte Università Parma, 2010.

Jammes, André. *Les Didot: Trois Siècles de Typographie & de Bibliographie 1698–1998*. Paris: Agence Culturelle de Paris, 1998.

Johnston, Alastair. *Transitional Faces: The Lives and Work of Richard Austin, Type-Cutter, and Richard Turner Austin, Wood Engraver*. Berkeley, CA: The Poltroon Press, 2013.

Mosley, James. "'Scotch Roman': What It Is & How It Got Its Name" in *The Ampersand*, vol. 17, nos. 3–4 (1998).

FAT FACE

Clough, James. "The Italian Monstrosity" in *TipoItalia* no. 1 (2008).

Gray, Nicolete. *Nineteenth Century Ornamented Typefaces*. Berkeley and Los Angeles: University of California Press, 1976.

Twyman, Michael. "The Bold Idea: The Use of Bold-Looking Types in the Nineteenth Century" in *Journal of the Printing Historical Society* no. 22 (1993).

SLAB SERIF

Kindel, Eric. "Stencil Dies: New Tools for an Old Trade" in Blume, J. et al, eds. *Vom Buch auf die Strasse: Grosse Schrift im öffentlichen Raum*. Leipzig: Hochschule für Grafik und Buchkunst: Leipzig, 2014.

WOOD TYPE

Gray, Nicolete. *Nineteenth Century Ornamented Typefaces*. Berkeley and Los Angeles: University of California Press, 1976.

Kelly, Rob Roy. *Wood Type: 1828-1900: Notes on the Evolution of Decorated and Large Types*. New York: Van Nostrand Reinhold, 1969.

LATE VICTORIAN TYPES

Clouse, Doug. *MacKellar, Smiths & Jordan: Typographic Tastemakers of the Late Nineteenth Century*. New Castle, DE: Oak Knoll Press, 2008.

Nash, Ray. "Ornamental Types in America" in *Nineteenth Century Ornamented Typefaces* by Nicolete Gray. Berkeley and Los Angeles: University of California Press, 1976.

Nebehay, Christian M. *Secession: Kataloge und Plakate der Wiener Secession 1898–1905*. Vienna: Edition Tusch, 1986.

Peterson, William S. "The Type-Designs of William Morris." *Journal of the Printing Historical Society*, nos. 19–20 (1985-87).

20TH CENTURY SERIFFED TYPES

Bringhurst, Robert. *Palatino: The Natural History of a Typeface*. San Francisco: The Book Club of California, 2016.

DaBoll, Raymond, ed. *The Book of Oz Cooper: An Appreciation of Oswald Bruce Cooper*. Chicago: The Society of Typographic Arts, 1949.

Goudy, Frederic W. *A Half-Century of Type Design and Typography, 1895-1945*. New York: The Typophiles, 1946. 2 vols.

Halbey, Hans, ed. *Gudrun Zapf von Hesse*. Leipzig: Gesellschaft zur Förderung der Druckkunst, 2002.

Harling, Robert. *The Letterforms and Type Designs of Eric Gill*. London: Eva Svensson and the Westerham Press, 1976.

Osterer, Heidrun and Philipp Stamm. *Adrian Frutiger Typefaces: The Complete Works*. Basel: Birkhauser Architecture, 2014. Rev. ed.

Zapf, Hermann. *About Alphabets: Some Marginal Notes on Type Design*. New York: The Typophiles, 1960.

GROTESQUES & GOTHICS

Homola, Wolfgang. "Type Design in the Age of the Machine. The 'Breite Grotesk' by J. G. Schelter & Giesecke" (MA thesis, University of Reading, 2004).

Mosley, James. *The Nymph and the Grot: The Revival of the Sanserif Letter*. London: Friends of the St. Bride Printing Library, 1999.

Pool, Albert-Jan. "Interview with Mr. DIN" in Lupi Asensio et al. *I Love DIN*. Hong Kong: Victionary, 2011.

Soskolne, Sara. "Sans Serif: The Early Years. Its Evolution as a Bicameral Style" (MA thesis, University of Reading, 2003).

GEOMETRIC SANS SERIFS

Brüning, Ute, ed. *Das A und O des Bauhauses*. Leipzig: Bauhaus-Archiv Edition, 1995.

Burke, Christopher. *Paul Renner: The Art of Typography*. London: Hyphen Press, 1998.

Dumas de Rauly, Alexandre and Michel Wlassikoff. *Futura: Une Gloire Typographique*. Paris: Éditions Norma, 2011.

Fleischmann, Gerd, ed. *Bauhaus Typografie: Drucksachen, Typografie, Reklame*. Berkeley, California: Gingko Press, 1997.

Heller, Steven and Louise Fili. *Deco Type: Stylish Alphabets of the '20s & '30s*. San Francisco: Chronicle Books, 1997.

HUMANIST SANS SERIFS

Gray, Nicolete. *Sans Serif and Other Experimental Lettering of the Early Renaissance*. New York and Seattle: LetterPerfect, 1997. Reprinted from Motif 5 (1960).

Harling, Robert. *The Letterforms and Type Designs of Eric Gill*. London: Eva Svensson and the Westerham Press, 1976.

Shaw, Paul. "Linotype Syntax." Unpublished, 2007.

Zapf, Hermann. *About Alphabets: Some Marginal Notes on Type Design*. New York: The Typophiles, 1960.

SCRIPTS

Chamaret, Sandra, Julien Gineste and Sébastien Morlighem. *Roger Excoffon et la Fonderie Olive*. Paris: Ypsilon Éditeur, 2010.

Henning, William E., ed. Paul Melzer. *An Elegant Hand: The Golden Age of Penmanship & Calligraphy*. New Castle, DE: Oak Knoll Press, 2002.

Osley, A. S. *Luminario: An Introduction to the Italian Writing-Books of the Sixteenth and Seventeenth Centuries*. Nieuwkoop: MIland Publishers, 1972.

Sull, Michael R. *Spencerian Script and Ornamental Penmanship*. Prairie Village, Kansas: LDG Publishing, 1989. 2 vols.

Index

Credits

American Printing History Association: p. 178; Michael Babock, Interrobang Press: p. 172; Stan Bevington: p. 174; Robert Bringhurst: p. 170; Christopher Burke: p. 214; James Clough: pp. 190, 220; Doug Clouse, p. 156; Columbia University Rare Book and Manuscript Library: front cover, back cover, pp. viii, 14, 32, 34, 40, 42, 46, 48, 51, 52, 56, 60, 64, 70, 73, 80, 83, 88, 90, 92, 94, 98, 103, 104, 105, 108, 111, 112, 116, 118 (left), 120, 122, 124, 126, 128, 146, 150, 152, 158, 164, 166, 191, 192, 196, 198, 236, 238, 240, Colophon; Columbia University, Avery Architectural & Fine Arts Library: p. 86; Dartmouth College, Rauner Library: p. 11; *Eye* magazine: frontispiece; Getty Images: p. 160; Julien Gineste: pp. 234, 242; Robert Green: p. 5; Hamilton Wood Type Museum: pp. 132, 145; Jonathan Hoefler: pp. 142, 144, 194; Eric Kindel: pp. 130, 131; Richard Kindersley: p. 20; John Lane: p. 78; Lars Müller Publishers: p. 204; Kent Lew: p. 218; Linotype: p. 30; Monotype Imaging: Contents, p. 228; Philip Moorhouse: p. 7; Museo Bodoniano: pp. 4, 5; The National Gallery of Art, Washington, DC: p. 24; Newberry Library, pp. 18, 26, 182; New York Public Library, Rare Book Division: p. 154; New York Public Library Digital Collection: p. 118 (right); Riccardo Olocco: p. 6; Massimo Pesce: p. 30; Albert-Jan Pool: p. 200; Providence Public Library, Daniel Berkeley Updike Collection on the History of Printing (Jordan Goffin): pp. 66, 114; Paul Shaw: pp. 2, 4, 5, 8, 13, 22, 28, 68, 100, 176, 180, 184, 203, 211, 222, 223, 232, 243; St. Bride's Institute, London: frontispiece; University of Amsterdam Library, Special Collections: pp. 186, 206, 216; University of Glasgow, The Hunterian Art Gallery: p. 162; University of Reading Library, Special Collections: p. 134; Unknown: pp. 38, 202; and Hermann Zapf, pp. 168, 170, 226, 230

About the author

Paul Shaw is a graphic designer and design historian. He teaches at Parsons School of Design, the School of Visual Arts, and the California Rare Book School. He is the author of *Helvetica and the New York City Subway System* (2009) and *Philip Grushkin: A Designer's Archive* (2013), editor of *The Eternal Letter: Two Millennia of the Classical Roman Capital* (2014), and co-editor of *Blackletter: Type and National Identity* (1999). Paul was the editor of *Codex: A Journal of Letterforms* and writes on type and lettering for *Eye*, *Print*, and *Baseline*. The American Institute of Graphic Arts, the Type Directors Club, and the Art Directors Club have honored his design work. He is the designer or co-designer of eighteen typefaces.

Acknowledgements

This book would not have been possible without the help of many individuals and instititutions. I received useful information and important advice from Paul Barnes, Roger Black, Robert Bringhurst, Christopher Burke, James Clough, Julien Gineste, Robert Green, Otmar Hoefer, Jonathan Hoefler, Richard Kegler, Eric Kindel, John Lane, David Lemon, Kent Lew, Mathieu Lommen, Rod McDonald, Philip Moorhouse, Sébastien Morlighem, James Mosley, Riccardo Olocco, Massimo Pesce, Albert-Jan Pool, Jean François Porchez, Christian Schwartz, David Shields, Mark Simonson, Fred Smeijers, Gerard Unger, and Mark van Bronkhorst. For images I am particularly indebted to Jane Siegel and Kevin O'Connor in the Rare Book and Manuscript Library at Columbia University for helping to locate material; and to the hardworking staff of the library's Preservation and Digital Conversion Divison (Emily Holmes, David Ortiz, Rebecca Haggerty and the techs behind the cameras) for handling my voluminous requests in a speedy manner. I would also like to thank Michael Babcock of Interrobang Letterpress, Lauren VanNest of the Newberry Library, Jordan Goffin of the Providence Public Library, Laura Weill of the University of Reading Library, and Stephanie Carpenter of the Hamilton Wood Type Museum for filling in important image gaps.

Most importantly, I wish to thank all of those at the foundries who provided typefaces for inclusion in this book: Adobe Systems (David Lemon and Christopher Slye), Alphabets Inc. (Peter Fraterdeus), Alter Littera (Jose Alberto Mauricio), American Type Founders (Mark van Bronkhorst), CanadaType (Patrick Griffin), Carter & Cone (Matthew Carter), Commercial Type (Paul Barnes and Christian Schwartz), Dennis Ortiz-Lopez Typefoundry (Dennis Ortiz-Lopez), Dutch Type Library (Frank Blokland), Elsner + Flake (Veronika Elsner), Emigre (Rudy VanderLans and Zuzana Licko), The Enschedé Font Foundry (Peter Matthias Noordzij), Expert Alphabets (Charles Nix), Feliciano Type Foundry (Mario Feliciano), The Font Bureau (Harry Parker), FontShop (Jürgen Siebert and Angie Poon), The Foundry (Freda Sack), Hamilton Wood Type Foundry (Richard Kegler), Hoefler & Co. (Jonathan Hoefler and Sara Soskolne), Lanston Type Company (Richard Kegler), LetterPerfect (Garrett Boge), Linotype (Otmar Hoefer and Akira Kobayashi), Mark Simonson Studio (Mark Simonson), Monotype Imaging (Allan Haley, Dan Rhatigan and Toshi Omigari), MvB Fonts (Mark van Bronkhorst), MyFonts (John Collins), OurType (Fred Smeijers and Corina Cotorobi), P22 (Richard Kegler), Rosetta Type Foundry (David Brezina), Storm Type Foundry (František Štorm), Sudtipos (Alejandro Paul), Swiss Typefaces (Daniela Party), Type Together (Veronika Burian), Typespec (Robert Green), Typofonderie (Jean François Porchez), Gerard Unger, and Village (Chester Jenkins). Without the help of these individuals and companies this book would not exist at all.

Finally, I want to thank Abby Goldstein for her patience and hard work in making this book as beautiful and good as it is. Not only have her efforts been instrumental in realizing my design ideas for *Revival Type*, but her opinions, advice and feedback on its contents have been equally invaluable. She has been a true collaborator.

Colophon

DESIGN: Abby Goldstein and Paul Shaw

PRODUCTION ASSISTANCE: Mara Sachs

TYPEFACES: Capitolium, Big Vesta and Vesta, all by Gerard Unger. Capitolium was designed by Unger in 1997 as part of a competition to create a wayfinding and information system for the city of Rome. The job was done in collaboration with n|p|k Industrial Design of Leiden. The typeface was inspired by an alphabet (left) by Giovan Francesco Cresci shown in his manual *Essemplare di piu sorti lettere* (1560).

ABCDEFGHIJKLMNOPQRSTUVWXYZ&ABCDEFGHIJKLMNO
PQRSTUVWXYZabcdefghijklmnopqrstuvwxyzffffififlfffiffl
1234567890123456789o{[(.,;:!?*)]}¶